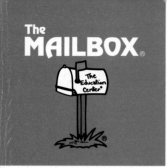

The MAILBOX

W9-BBM-006

THE BEST OF The MAILBOX MAGAZINE

The Best of MAILBOX

PRESCHOOL

The best activities from the 2003–2006 issues of *The Mailbox*® magazine

- ★ Arts-and-Crafts Ideas
- ★ Bulletin Boards & Displays
- ★ Circle-Time Activities
- ★ Learning Center Ideas

- ★ Literacy Activities
- ★ Math Activities
- ★ Thematic Units
- ★ Seasonal Activities

Topic and Skills Index on page 190!

Managing Editor: Jenny Chapman

Editorial Team: Becky S. Andrews, Diane Badden, Kimberley Bruck, Karen A. Brudnak, Kitty Campbell, Pam Crane, Lynette Dickerson, Tazmen Hansen, Marsha Heim, Lori Z. Henry, Sheila Krill, Debra Liverman, Dorothy C. McKinney, Thad H. McLaurin, Sharon Murphy, Jennifer Nunn, Mark Rainey, Hope Rodgers, Becky Saunders

www.themailbox.com

©2008 The Mailbox®
All rights reserved.
ISBN10 #1-56234-834-5 • ISBN13 #978-156234-834-2

Except as provided for herein, no part of this publication may be reproduced or transmitted in any form or by any means, electronic or mechanical, including photocopying, recording, or storing in any information storage and retrieval system or electronic online bulletin board, without prior written permission from The Education Center, Inc. Permission is given to the original purchaser to reproduce patterns and reproducibles for individual classroom use only and not for resale or distribution. Reproduction for an entire school or school system is prohibited. Please direct written inquiries to The Education Center, Inc., P.O. Box 9753, Greensboro, NC 27429-0753. The Education Center®, *The Mailbox*®, the mailbox/post/grass logo, and The Mailbox Book Company® are registered trademarks of The Education Center, Inc. All other brand or product names are trademarks or registered trademarks of their respective companies.

Manufactured in the United States
10 9 8 7 6 5 4 3 2 1

Table of Contents

Arts & Crafts for Little Hands

Arts & Crafts for Little Hands

"A-peel-ing" Apples

You can count on little ones really tearing into these apples! To make one, tear a 9" x 12" sheet of red construction paper into pieces. Glue the resulting apple peels onto a precut apple shape (cut from a nine-inch square of white construction paper). Tear a stem shape from brown paper and a leaf shape from green paper. Glue the stem and leaf in place, and the apple is ready for display.

Kellie Shaner-Gordner—PreK
D & K's Youngland
Hughesville, PA

Too Cute Turtles!

These reptiles are simply irresistible! To make the shell, paint one side of a nine-inch square of bubble wrap the color of your choice. Press the painted side of the wrap onto a nine-inch square of white construction paper. When the paint is dry, cut a large circular turtle shell from the paper. Next, cut out a turtle head, a tail, and four legs from construction paper. Use crayons to add desired details to the cutouts and then glue the cutouts under the rim of the shell. There you have it! A turtle that is just too cute!

Diane Muldoon—Three-Year-Olds
St. Matthew's Nursery School
Maple Glen, PA

Footprint Ghosts

Your little ones will want to step right up and create these gorgeous ghosts! Paint the bottom of a child's foot with white tempera paint. Then have him carefully step onto a sheet of black or purple construction paper. When the paint dries, have him use a black marker to add eyes and a mouth to his ghost print. Ooh!

Ann Zelter and Jenny Knoll—Toddlers
Salem Lutheran Preschool
Springville, NY

Preschool Pumpkins

These pumpkins are *cute!* Give each child a small foam ball that has been flattened on one side by pressing it against a table. Have her glue pieces of orange tissue paper all over the ball, being sure to overlap the pieces. When the glue is dry, help the child stick a two-inch piece of green pipe cleaner into the top of her pumpkin to create a stem. Then, if desired, have her draw eyes, a nose, and a mouth on her pumpkin with a black marker. Display these pumpkins for everyone to admire!

Stacy Beman—Toddlers
Plaza Boulevard Child Development Center
Rapid City, SD

Candy Cane

Dreidel

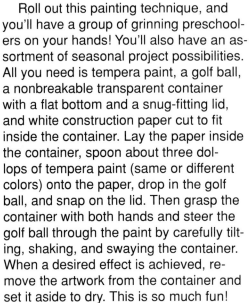

Unity Cup

Shake, Rattle, and Roll!

Roll out this painting technique, and you'll have a group of grinning preschoolers on your hands! You'll also have an assortment of seasonal project possibilities. All you need is tempera paint, a golf ball, a nonbreakable transparent container with a flat bottom and a snug-fitting lid, and white construction paper cut to fit inside the container. Lay the paper inside the container, spoon about three dollops of tempera paint (same or different colors) onto the paper, drop in the golf ball, and snap on the lid. Then grasp the container with both hands and steer the golf ball through the paint by carefully tilting, shaking, and swaying the container. When a desired effect is achieved, remove the artwork from the container and set it aside to dry. This is so much fun!

Nancy Goldberg—3-Year-Olds
B'nai Israel Schilit Nursery School
Rockville, MD

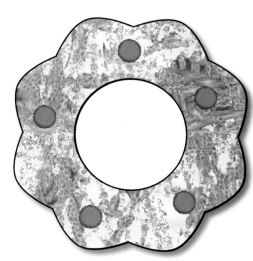

Wreath

Star of David

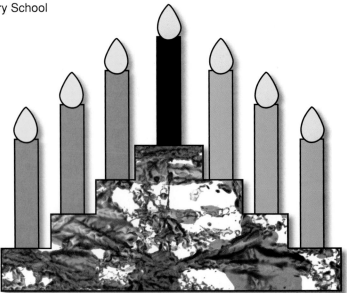

Kinara

Nose So Bright!

Even a nighttime blizzard can't stop Rudolph's bright red nose from leading the way! Squeeze white tempera paint onto a paper plate and provide a clean and empty 20-ounce plastic soft drink bottle. To make a blizzard of snowflakes, dip the bottom of the bottle into the paint and randomly stamp it onto a sheet of black construction paper. Repeat the process until a desired effect is achieved. Then dip a red pom-pom into glue and press it onto the painted paper. Santa's on his way!

Snazzy Snow Globe

The forecast for this snow globe project is a flurry of excitement! In advance, cut an assortment of snowpals from holiday gift wrap and then, for each child, cut out two same-size circles—one from clear Con-Tact covering and one from blue construction paper. To make the globe, peel the backing from the circle of clear covering and lay the circle on a table, sticky side up. Press a snowpal cutout facedown on the sticky surface and then press small pieces of torn white paper around the snowpal. Next, align a blue circle atop the artwork and press it into place. To make the snow globe's base, cut a half circle from brown or black paper and glue the globe to it as shown. Let it snow!

Lois Maiese—Multiage Class
Camden County College Child Care Center
Blackwood, NJ

Lovebugs

Welcome Valentine's Day with these colorful critters adorning your classroom! To prepare, cut out the following shapes for each child: a large oval from pink construction paper (body), two smaller ovals from waxed paper (wings), and six thin strips from purple construction paper (legs). Have each child glue a pair of wings to the lovebug's body and then glue on six legs. Invite her to use a red or purple crayon to draw a face on her lovebug. Cute!

adapted from an idea by Cindy Paolucci
and Lynn Lavelle
Warren Community Elementary—LEAP Preschool
W. Warren, MA

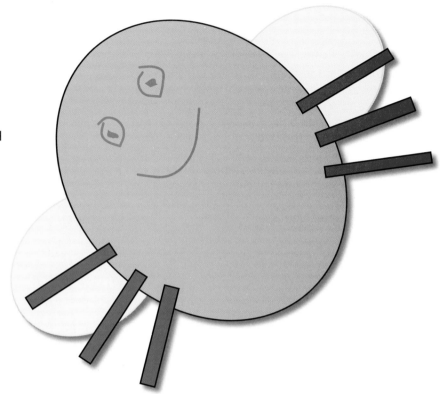

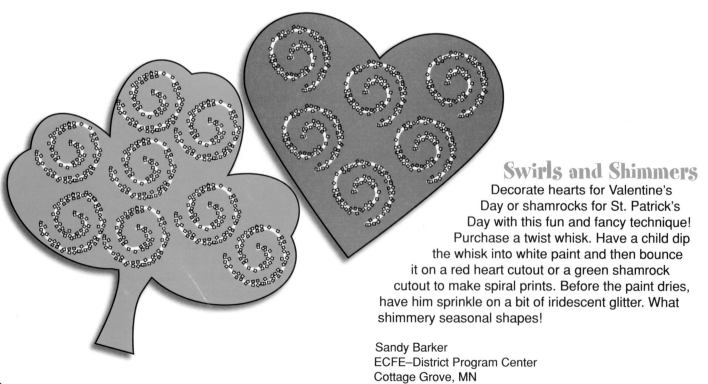

Swirls and Shimmers

Decorate hearts for Valentine's Day or shamrocks for St. Patrick's Day with this fun and fancy technique! Purchase a twist whisk. Have a child dip the whisk into white paint and then bounce it on a red heart cutout or a green shamrock cutout to make spiral prints. Before the paint dries, have him sprinkle on a bit of iridescent glitter. What shimmery seasonal shapes!

Sandy Barker
ECFE–District Program Center
Cottage Grove, MN

Buzzy Little Bees

A potato masher is the key to making these adorable bees! Dip a potato masher into a shallow pan of black tempera paint. Then press the masher on a yellow sheet of construction paper. Continue in the same way to make several bees. When the paint is dry, glue tissue paper wings and a construction paper eye to each bee. Then use a black marker to further embellish the scene. There's sure to be quite a buzz about these cute projects!

Sandy Barker
Early Childhood Family Education
Cottage Grove, MN

Beautiful Bubbles

After an experience making bubbles with bubble solution, invite students to make these lovely pieces of art! Gather yarn in different shades of blue; then snip the yarn into different lengths. To make a bubble picture, brush a thick layer of glue on a sheet of tagboard. Then place pieces of yarn on the glue, carefully shaping the yarn into circles to resemble bubbles.

Michelle Freed
Peru State College
Peru, NE

9

Splendid Sea Horse

This craft would be an excellent addition to an ocean-themed mural! Make a construction paper sea horse cutout. Draw an eye on the sea horse. Then glue pieces of crepe paper streamer around the edge of the pattern, including three longer strips as shown. Finally, glue crumpled brown tissue paper pieces to the sea horse's body.

Kim Dessel
Pixie Preschool and Kindergarten
Spotswood, NJ

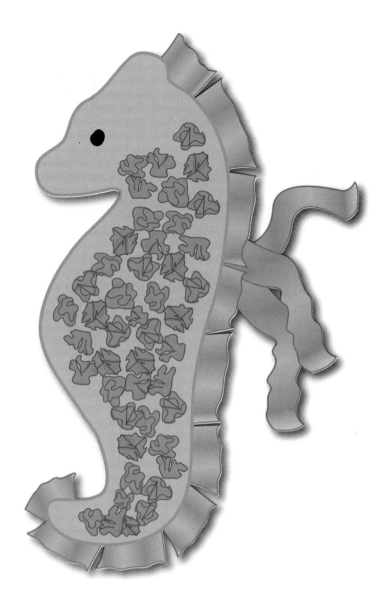

Totally Texturized!

When this paint dries, it has a unique texture that little ones will be eager to touch. To make the paint, mix six cups of flour with three cups of water. Separate the mixture into several different containers. Then use tempera paint to tint each container a different color. Use your fingers to spread a different color of paint on each of two construction paper circles. When the paint is dry, glue the circles over a construction paper cone to resemble scoops of ice cream.

Anne Salajekeh
St. Mary Queen of Angels
Swartz Creek, MI

Fabulous Fireworks!

Cut a supply of cotton swabs in half. Place red, white, and blue tempera paint in separate containers. Mix a small amount of white glue with each color of paint. To make fabulous fireworks, dip the end of a prepared cotton swab in a desired paint color; then place the swab on a sheet of black construction paper. Continue in the same way, placing the swabs in an arrangement similar to the one shown to resemble fireworks. When a desired effect is achieved, sprinkle gold glitter over the swabs. What a fantastic fireworks display!

Camille Cooper
Emporia State University Center for Early Childhood Education
Emporia, KS

Cool Castle

Use building blocks to make two-dimensional sandcastles! Place several building blocks in a shallow tray of brown tempera paint. Then remove a block and press it on a sheet of construction paper. Continue in the same way with other blocks to make a castle. Then sprinkle sand over the wet paint. When the paint is dry, brush off the excess sand. Waves won't be able to knock down this splendid sandcastle!

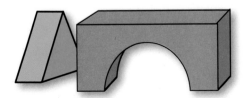

Salty Shapes

This concoction of glue, salt, and watercolor paint will make super cool shapes! First, have a child slowly squeeze a bottle of white glue to create a basic shape on a sheet of tagboard. Place the sheet in a shallow box; then sprinkle a generous amount of salt. Lightly shake off the excess salt. Then have a child dip a paintbrush into water and then into watercolor paint. Have her gently touch the paintbrush to her glue and salt shape. Watch her delight as the paint spreads into the mixture, coloring her shape!

Squish!

Recycle some common items to make some painting tools that are perfect for preschool! Cut a number of three-inch circles from plastic lids. Hot-glue each one onto an old thread spool or empty film canister. Have a child drop a few blobs of different colors of paint onto a sheet of paper. Then have her squish the paint with the homemade squishers! Watch as the colors blend into a beautiful painting.

Ann Marie Einfeldt
Tot Spot Child Care
Brighton, MI

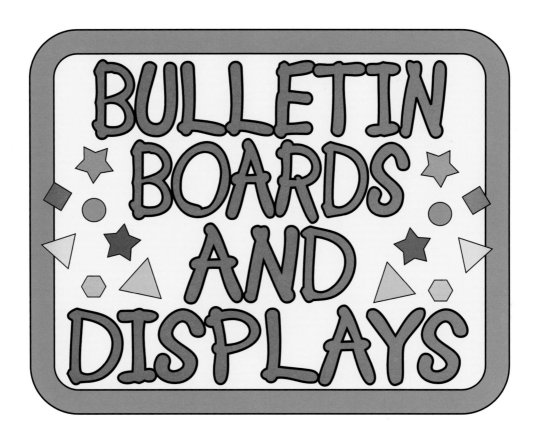

BULLETIN BOARDS AND DISPLAYS

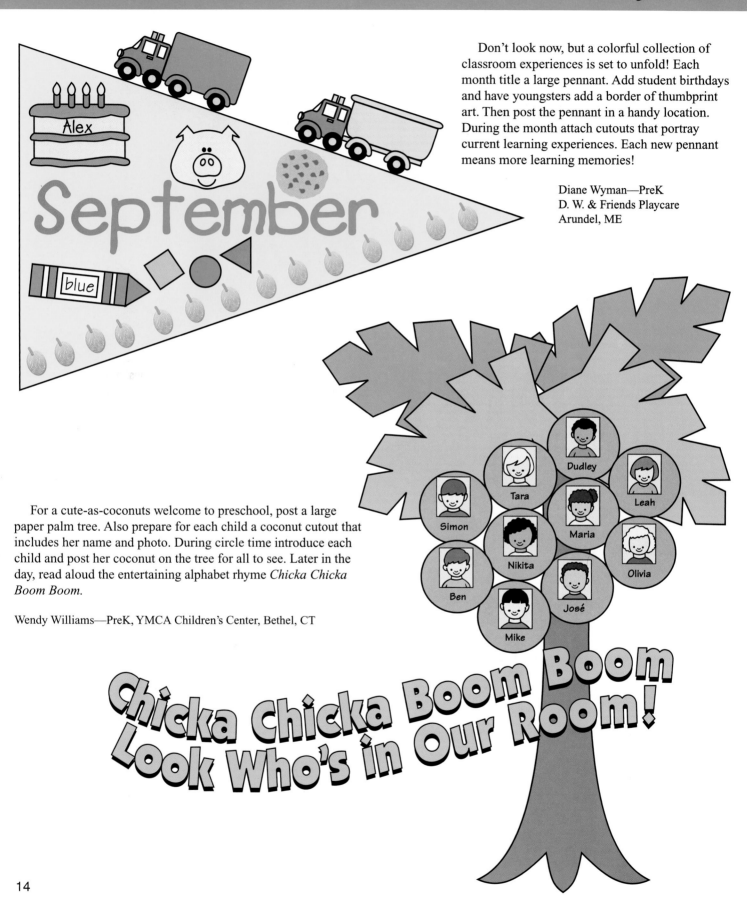

Don't look now, but a colorful collection of classroom experiences is set to unfold! Each month title a large pennant. Add student birthdays and have youngsters add a border of thumbprint art. Then post the pennant in a handy location. During the month attach cutouts that portray current learning experiences. Each new pennant means more learning memories!

Diane Wyman—PreK
D. W. & Friends Playcare
Arundel, ME

For a cute-as-coconuts welcome to preschool, post a large paper palm tree. Also prepare for each child a coconut cutout that includes her name and photo. During circle time introduce each child and post her coconut on the tree for all to see. Later in the day, read aloud the entertaining alphabet rhyme *Chicka Chicka Boom Boom.*

Wendy Williams—PreK, YMCA Children's Center, Bethel, CT

Chicka Chicka Boom Boom Look Who's in Our Room!

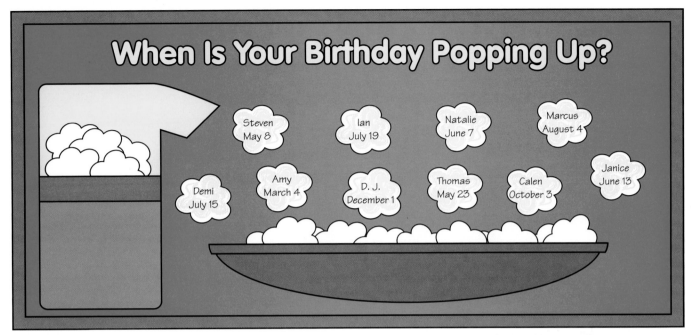

When Is Your Birthday Popping Up?

Steven
May 8

Ian
July 19

Natalie
June 7

Marcus
August 4

Demi
July 15

Amy
March 4

D. J.
December 1

Thomas
May 23

Calen
October 3

Janice
June 13

Spotlight youngsters' birthdays on popcorn cutouts! Attach cutouts of a simple bowl and a hot-air popcorn popper to a bulletin board. Give each child a white popcorn cutout. Have each child sponge-paint his cutout yellow to make it appear as if it's been buttered. When the paint is dry, write each child's name and birthdate on his cutout. Mount the popcorn on the board; then add the title shown. What an eye-popping display!

Heather Campbell, HCDS, Pennington, NJ

Celebrate your student of the week with a "dino-mite" display! Label several copies of a dinosaur footprint with a different prompt as shown. Have the student of the week dictate to complete each prompt and then add a drawing. Attach the footprints, photos brought by the child, and a dinosaur cutout to a board titled as shown. When it's time to change the display, staple the footprints together to make a take-home keepsake for the child!

inspired by an idea from Melinda Blackwill
Hays Head Start
Hays, KS

A "Dino-mite" Student!

Samantha
Murphy

My favorite
color is <u>pink</u>.

My favorite food
is <u>spaghetti</u>.

My favorite
animal is <u>a cat</u>.

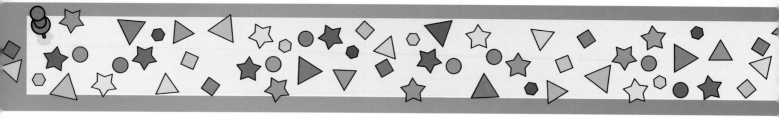

We Have Lots to Crow About!

I have a new baby sister.

I like bananas.

I went to the dentist.

I went to the fire station.

My dog got a flea.

My dad broke his toe.

My brother has a girlfriend. Yuck!

My cat had kittens!

Couple a covey of cute crows with your students' snapshots and comments to make a display that creates a lot of talk! To make the crows, help each child press one footprint and two handprints on a strip of white paper as shown. (Use washable tempera.) Later, attach hole-reinforcement eyes and paper beaks. Display the crows, snapshots, and your youngsters' dictated comments. Now you're talkin'!

Susan Polojac—PreK, Greensburg YMCA Y-Tots, Greensburg, PA

Welcome to our Preschool Patch!

Preschoolers and pumpkins go hand in hand at this colorful display! To make the pumpkins, have little ones tear orange paper into small pieces and glue the pieces onto precut pumpkin shapes. Then, using washable tempera paint, help each child press a handprint leaf on white paper. When the prints are dry, cut them out. Post the projects along a vine of green yarn. Impressive!

Jo Ann B. Stock—Three- and Four-Year-Olds, Rainbow Preschool, Stockton, CA

Light up your classroom this season with a display of Rudolph's red-nosed friends! First, tape a string of Christmas lights with red bulbs across your board, making sure the plug reaches an outlet. For each reindeer, trace a child's shoe and both hands. Cut out the tracings and attach the hand-shaped antlers to the shoe cutout. Have the child add eyes and a mouth. Then cut a hole for the nose and attach the reindeer over a bulb at its base. Ho, ho, ho—what a glow!

Michael Marks
Harding Elementary
Lebanon, PA

Craft a batch of gingerbread people for this yummy display! Have each child decorate a brown construction paper cookie person with rickrack, yarn, ribbon, paper reinforcements, craft foam shapes, or paper punches. Display the finished cookies on aluminum baking sheets or large pieces of aluminum foil.

Pam Sartory, City of Palm Beach Gardens Recreation Dept., Palm Beach Gardens, FL

Happy Birthday, Dr. King!

Nigel   Maria   Alex   Theo   Joseph   Grace   Leon   Max   Nia   Kym   Tan

You can't help but smile when you look at this birthday display! And wouldn't that have made Martin Luther King Jr. proud? Assist each child in making a self-portrait from gathered supplies. Provide skin-toned paper for the project or blend paint colors to create skin tones. Then ask each child to write (or trace an outline of) his name on a birthday banner like the one shown. It's true—smiles are contagious!

Check out the shapes on these snowpals! For an interactive exhibit, display two poster board snowpals (with arms and earmuff bands) within your youngsters' reach. Replace each shape detail pictured with an adhesive Velcro hook fastener. From colorful tagboard, cut two or more sets of shapes and attach an adhesive Velcro loop fastener to the back of each cutout. Students will have a flurry of fun adding shapely details to these snow buddies!

adapted from an idea by
Pam Ingram
Davenport A+ School
Lenoir, NC

Warm the hearts of classroom visitors with a heartfelt and handcrafted valentine greeting! Glue a photo of each child to a heart cutout. Then ask each youngster to decorate his cutout to his heart's desire! Also trace the students' hands onto paper and cut out the resulting hand shapes. Showcase the handiwork as shown. Love is definitely in the air!

Pam Vannatta—Preschool, Kids N Kapers, Lexington, KY

Students are sure to find these colorful shapes especially interesting! After all, the shapes are made from their artwork! With your youngsters' permission, cut samples of their easel artwork into desired shapes. Then use the cutouts to create a display like the one shown. Plan to periodically update the artwork. Shapes are so cool!

Jo Ann B. Stock—Preschool
Rainbow School
Stockton, CA

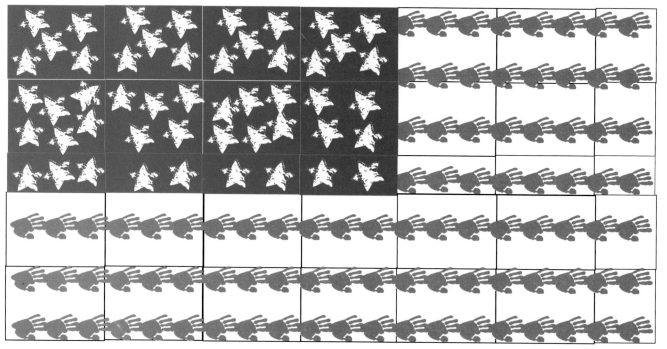

Ready to step into summer? For each child, cut the shape of a shoe sole from white construction paper. Have the child paint or color the cutout as desired; then punch three holes as shown and thread pipe cleaners through the holes. Label each completed flip-flop with the child's name and the year. Then add the flip-flops and title to the board.

Brenda Watkins, Playhouse Child Care Center, Henderson, NC
Jennifer McDonald, Creative World Preschool, Wilmington, NC

What a glorious Old Glory! For this giant flag, have youngsters paint large pieces of white paper blue. Use these to form the field of blue and then sponge-paint fifty white stars on it. Have youngsters make red handprints on white paper for the flag's stripes. Assemble the flag on a bulletin board for a super salute to the USA!

Debbie Vrana, Jefferson Elementary, Princeton, IL

Creative Learning
Experiences
for Little Hands

BUSY HANDS

BUSY HANDS

Creative Learning Experiences for Little Hands

NIFTY NEWSPAPER USES

Here's a news flash! Newspaper is neat for all kinds of motor skills practice!

ideas by Lucia Kemp Henry, Fallon, NV

NEWSPAPER COLLAGE

Ripping and tearing are required for this artistic newspaper activity! Demonstrate for little ones how to tear a sheet of newspaper into strips. Encourage each child to experiment with tearing strips of different widths. After youngsters have torn a supply of strips, mix equal parts of water and liquid starch. Have each child dip each strip in the mixture and then slide her fingers along the strip to remove the excess liquid. Then instruct her to place the strip on a 12" x 18" sheet of construction paper in any fashion she likes. Encourage her to continue to add strips to her paper to make a unique collage. Invite each student to share her dried collage with the group. Then attach the collages to a bulletin board and title the display "Nifty Newspaper Collages!"

PAPER SCRUNCH

Want students to strengthen their fine-motor skills? Try this idea! To begin, have each child lay a half sheet of a newspaper (12" x 22") on a table. Instruct her to place the palm of her hand on the center of the paper. Then have her use only her fingers to scrunch the paper together until she has gathered it up in her hand, making a ball. Encourage each youngster to try this task with her other hand too. Then challenge little ones to repeat the activity with larger pieces of newspaper. Have students toss the newspaper balls in a box to use with "Painting With Newspaper" on page 23. Scrunch, scrunch!

PAINTING WITH NEWSPAPER

Use newspaper balls as stand-ins for sponge printers in this easy painting activity! To prepare, crumple newspaper into balls or use the paper balls from "Paper Scrunch" on page 22. Also cut newspaper into half sheets (12" x 22"). At your painting center, have each child clip a newspaper page to his easel. Then instruct him to grasp a newspaper ball, dip it in paint, and press it repeatedly on his paper to make prints. Invite him to repeat the printing process with a fresh newspaper ball and a different color of paint. After he finishes painting, have each student place his paint-dipped newspaper balls in the trash. Display the paintings along with the title "Crumple, Dip, Print, Print, Print!"

SHREDDED PAPER SENSORY SEARCH

Turn your sand table into a great sensory experience. Shred newspaper with a paper shredder to make enough filler for your empty sand table. Then hide consecutive numbers of spring objects in the newspaper, such as one plush bunny toy, two gardening gloves, three plastic flowerpots, four silk flowers, five seed packets, and six plastic chicks. Make a numbered picture key on chart paper and display it next to the table. Encourage each student who visits the center to use her sense of touch to explore the table's contents to find all the items on the chart. Happy spring, and happy searching!

NEWSPAPER TOSS

Making these beanbags is a snap! Shred newspaper with a paper shredder to make a large supply. Give each child a resealable plastic bag. Have her fill her bag with shredded newspaper. Before sealing each child's bag with clear packing tape, drop in three or four jingle bells. Have youngsters decorate their bags with stickers if desired. Place a hoop on the floor and have students toss their bags in the hoop from varying distances. Ready, set, toss!

BUSY HANDS
Creative Learning Experiences for Little Hands

LOTS OF DOTS

Here a dot, there a dot! With explorations featuring bingo daubers, your little ones are sure to see lots of dots!

ideas contributed by Ada Goren, Winston-Salem, NC

FLIPPIN' FOR PANCAKES!

Place at a table a blue bingo dauber, a supply of tan construction paper pancakes, and pancake-related dramatic-play items, such as a skillet, a spatula, an empty syrup bottle, and plastic plates and forks. A youngster uses the dauber to make blue dots on several pancakes to resemble blueberries. Then he uses the props to cook up some breakfast-themed dramatic play!

DOUBLES AND TRIPLES

Use thick rubber bands to bind pairs of bingo daubers together. Then place the daubers and a supply of paper at a table. Encourage youngsters to explore making dots with these unique painting tools. When each student has had ample opportunity to investigate the dauber pairs, bind groups of three daubers together. These colossal painting tools are triple the fun!

Kwanzaa Candles

Cut a strip of white bulletin board paper and tape it to a tabletop. Then place at the table glue, yellow bingo daubers, a shallow container of water, and a supply of nine-inch construction paper strips (candles) in the following colors: red, green, and black. Each child glues several candles to the paper. Then she dips the tip of the dauber into the water and presses it above each candle to make the flame. Look at all the glowing lights!

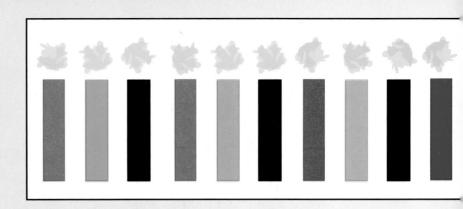

Dot-to-Dot

Place drawing paper, markers, and a selection of bingo daubers at a table. A child uses a bingo dauber to make several dots on a sheet of paper. Then she uses a variety of colorful markers to connect the dots. What a unique piece of modern art!

Beautiful Berries

Tape a length of bulletin board paper to a tabletop. Provide access to the following items: glue, a red bingo dauber, and a supply of green holly leaf cutouts. A youngster uses the bingo dauber to make a cluster of three berries. Then he glues holly leaves near the berries. When the paper is filled with holly and the glue is dry, attach the paper to a wall to make a festive decoration!

BUSY HANDS

Creative Learning Experiences for Little Hands

A BUBBLE BASH!

They're round, they pop, and they're full of air. They're big, they're small, and they're fun to share! What are they? Bubbles! Invite your preschoolers to explore the look and feel of bubbles with these activities!

by Sue Fleischmann—Child and Family Specialist
Waukesha County Project Head Start
Waukesha, WI

COOKIN' UP BUBBLES!

Put several cooking utensils in your water table and add a squirt or two of fragrant dish soap. Then watch your little ones cook up some bubbles! Try adding egg beaters, potato mashers, whisks, spatulas, measuring cups, measuring spoons, bowls, and cups. Bubble cake, anyone?

BUBBLE BOTTLES

Do water bubbles look like bubble-bath bubbles? Provide an assortment of bubble bottles and let your preschoolers judge! Collect a few 16-ounce clear plastic drink bottles. Remove the labels and keep the lids. Next, partially fill each bottle with a different noncarbonated liquid, such as water, bubble solution, vegetable oil, bubble bath, and baby shampoo. Hot-glue a lid on each bottle. Then invite your little ones to shake the bottles and observe the bubbles inside.

BUBBLES UNDERFOOT

This activity is sure to be "pop-ular" with your preschoolers! Use double-sided tape to adhere a large piece of bubble wrap (the kind with small bubbles works best) to your classroom floor. Also provide a tub of bubble wrap scraps nearby. Invite your little ones to walk over the fixed bubble wrap in their stocking feet! When they tire of that, suggest they each take a scrap of bubble wrap and try popping the bubbles using various body parts, such as fingers, elbows, and knees! Pop! Pop! Pop!

BUBBLING BREW

For a super sensory experience, add a touch of preschool chemistry to your youngsters' bubble investigations! At this adult-directed station, mix together one package (or one tablespoon) of yeast and one tablespoon of sugar in a clear bowl. Then add warm water and watch the bubbling begin! Invite youngsters to put their hands in the bubbling brew to feel it. What a delightful feeling—and a delicious smell too!

Amy Shimelman—PreK
JCAA Early Childhood Program
Austin, TX

SIZE AND SHAPE

Can bubbles be big or small? Can they be square or triangular? At this bubble-blowing station even the youngest bubble fan can discover the answers to these questions! Provide a shallow container of bubble solution and a variety of blowers, such as sections of cardboard tubes, a flyswatter, cookie cutters, and pipe cleaners bent into different shapes. Let the bubble making begin!

DOUBLE THE BUBBLES

It takes two to create these beauteous bubble masterpieces! Work closely with two students at a time. Give each partner a personalized sheet of white art paper, a clean drinking straw, and a small paper cup that contains a mixture of bubble solution and tempera paint. (Each partner's bubble solution must be tinted a different color.) Then ask each child to use her straw to blow air into her cup. When she's blown a fountain of bubbles, help her gently place her paper atop the bubbles. When each partner has captured two or three sets of bubbles on her own paper, have her trade papers with her partner and repeat the activity using her partner's paper. Double the bubbles, double the fun!

BUSY HANDS

Creative Learning Experiences for Little Hands

FABULOUS FEATHERS!

Feathers aplenty! Feathers galore! Feathers sure are lots of fun to explore!

ideas contributed by Ada Goren, Winston-Salem, NC

BEAUTIFUL BRUSHES

Gather several large craft feathers and place each feather in a shallow pan of tempera paint. Place the pans at your art table along with a supply of construction paper. A youngster writes his name on a sheet of paper. Then he glides the paint-covered feathers over the paper until a desired effect is achieved. How lovely!

FUN FEATHER SORT

To prepare for this exploration, make four copies of a bird pattern on different colors of construction paper. Cut out the birds. Then gather several craft feathers to match each bird and place them in a container. Place the birds and container at a center. A child visits the center and sorts the feathers on the matching birds!

Copy Cats

Following directions

Youngsters will think this activity is the cat's meow! For each child, make a paper headband with two cat-ear cutouts. Play a version of Follow the Leader by designating a cat leader and having everyone else play the copycats. Invite the leader to choose a cat action, such as purring, cleaning his paws, or meowing. Have all the copycats do the same. After a few kitty-cat moves, instruct the leader to lead the group to line up, wash their hands, or go back to their seats—whatever you need youngsters to do as you head into your next activity!

Deborah Ryan—Child and Family Development Specialist
Early Head Start
Milwaukie, OR

Daniel

Whose Name Is Hiding?

Identifying characteristics of one's name

Familiarize your students with one another's names with this hide-and-seek activity! Each day, choose a child and write his name on several sticky notes. Hide the notes throughout your classroom. Have your preschoolers hunt for the sticky notes and return them to your group area. Then post all of the notes on the wall or chalkboard and discuss the unique qualities of the child's name, such as its beginning letter and its length. Your little ones will know everyone's name in no time!

Dana Sanders—Preschool
Hamilton Crossing Elementary
Cartersville, GA

Carpet-Square Shapes

Identifying shapes

Reinforce the shapes your preschoolers are learning by arranging your circle-time seating to match! For example, when you are teaching your little ones about rectangles, arrange carpet squares in a large rectangle. Invite the class to look at the shape and then sit on the carpet squares. After your youngsters have mastered the shapes, try using carpet squares to form letters of the alphabet.

Tami Renner—PreK
Flanagan's Preschool
Collegeville, PA

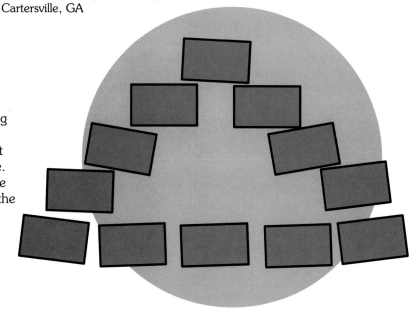

A Friendly Chant
Social awareness

Use this easy chant to help your new preschoolers get acquainted. Invite the child named in the third line to stand up and wave to the group when directed. As a variation, call out "girls," "boys," or the names of teachers or parent helpers in the third line.

Who are all our friends today?
Who is here to learn and play?
Stand up, [child's name], and look around.
Wave hello and sit back down.

Reggie Bender—Preschool
Orchard Park Cooperative Nursery School
Orchard Park, NY

A Colorful Concoction
Sorting by color

Stir up some interest in colors with a pot of color soup! To prepare, cut out various simple shapes from different colors of construction paper. Label a box or basket with each color. Then hide the colorful shapes throughout your classroom. At circle time, ask youngsters to hunt for the shapes and sort them by color into the containers. To conclude the activity, dump all the shapes into a large pot and invite little ones to take turns stirring the pot of color soup with a big wooden spoon!

Once youngsters know their colors, relabel the containers to help your students concentrate on the shapes and make a pot of shape soup instead!

Pepper Leclerc—PreK
Merrimack Valley Christian Day School
Lowell, MA

Day by Day
Increasing number recognition

Ho, ho, ho! This December, deliver a daily math lesson with a little help from Santa! Create a large Santa face like the one shown. On Santa's beard write desired calendar dates, beginning with 1. Post the cutout within students' reach. Each day, beginning on December 1, help one child glue a cotton ball on Santa's beard atop the current date. When previous dates are not covered, such as weekend dates, enlist more individuals to help. Your little ones' interest in numbers is sure to increase right along with the fluffiness of Santa's beard!

Carrie Whitney—PreK
Summit Academy
Middletown, KY

Closure Clips
Describing experiences

Conclude each day by asking little ones to describe their favorite experiences. For easy management, divide a large poster board circle into sections. Then program each section to reflect a different part of the school day. Also personalize a clothespin for each child. Begin by talking with students about the different things they did during the school day. Then have each child tell what he liked best and help him clip his clothespin to the corresponding section of the circle. You'll quickly discover that this activity encourages language development at school, and at home too!

Debbie Sharpe—Three- and Four-Year-Olds
Springfield Preschool
Springfield, CO

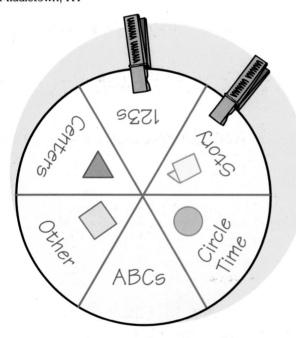

Letter Soup
Identifying letters

A pot of letter soup is perfect nourishment for letter identification skills! Keep a large pot, a supply of Ping-Pong balls, and a ladle handy. Each time you introduce an alphabet letter, write the letter on a Ping-Pong ball and put the ball in the pot. From time to time, bring out the soup pot. Have one child dip the ladle into the soup and scoop up a letter. After the letter is identified by the class, have youngsters do a quick search of the room looking for other examples of the letter. Repeat the activity several times. Then return the letters to the pot and set the pot aside until additional servings of letter soup are in order!

adapted from an idea by Joelle Quimby—Preschool
Kids & Kreations
New Berlin, WI

Dinosaur Roars

Following directions, experimenting with voice volume and tone

Little ones will have a roaring good time voicing a variety of dinosaur roars! In advance, help each child make a dinosaur stick puppet like the one shown. Then say the provided rhyme and invite students to roar like dinosaurs. Repeat the rhyme several times, each time replacing the underlined phrase with a different type of roar for students to make, such as *very soft, very high, very low, sad, silly, sleepy, wide awake, very fast,* and *very slow.* The possibilities are HUGE!

> Dinosaurs, dinosaurs, on the floor,
> Let me hear your [very loud] roar!

Sue Fleischmann—Child and Family Specialist
Waukesha County Project Head Start, Waukesha, WI

Tooth Fairy, Tooth Fairy

Observing and interpreting body language

Pearly whites are out-of-sight in this fun guessing game! Give one child a magic wand and have her play the part of the tooth fairy. While the tooth fairy covers her eyes, give another child a tooth cutout to hide in his lap. When the tooth is out of sight, have the tooth fairy uncover her eyes as her classmates chant, "Tooth Fairy, Tooth Fairy, who has the tooth?" After the tooth fairy guesses correctly (with clues if necessary), invite the child who was holding the tooth to be the tooth fairy for the next round.

Michele Menzel
Appleton, WI

Heart March and Match

Matching numerals and sets

Try this Valentine's Day variation of musical chairs! On pink construction paper trace one heart shape per child. Program half of each heart with a numeral and the remaining half with a corresponding set of hearts. Cut out the hearts and then cut each heart in half to separate its numeral from its heart set. Arrange chairs in a circle, one chair per child. On each chair lay the right half of a heart. Hand out the remaining heart halves and have preschoolers march around the chairs to music. When the music stops, each child finds a match for his heart half and sits down! To play again, each child places one half of his cutout in an empty chair. Then he trades his remaining heart half with a classmate.

Kathy Fraites—Three- and Four-Year-Olds
Redeemer Christian Nursery School, Ramsey, NJ

Which Season Is It?
Recognizing characteristics of different seasons
Draw little ones' attention to the characteristics of the seasons! Provide four calendar pictures, each of which clearly represents one of the four seasons. Have students describe what they see in each picture and invite them to share their thoughts about that time of the year. Then post the four pictures and invite each child to name his favorite season. If desired, write each child's name on a card and display the cards so that a class graph of your preschoolers' favorite time of year results!

adapted from an idea by Kathleen Sherbon
North County Christian School
Atascadero, CA

Bunny Hop
Recognizing numbers
Put a seasonal twist on number recognition with an activity that keeps youngsters hopping! Program ten large cards with the numerals 1–10. Then draw a simple bunny on each of four additional cards. To play, show one card at a time. Encourage students to name the number they see. When they see a card with a bunny on it, they first say, "Bunny hop!" Then they hop up and sit right back down. Keep the numbers coming and the hopping going as long as your students' interest—and energy—lasts!

Danielle Wieging—Preschool
Broadway Kids Place
Spencerville, OH

Letter Hunt
Matching letters, introducing alphabetical order
Add a literacy element to an Easter egg hunt! To prepare, cut 26 egg shapes from pastel construction paper or wallpaper samples. Label each egg with a different letter. When your preschoolers are out of the room, hide the eggs. Also roll out a long strip of bulletin board paper on which you've written the alphabet.

At group time, encourage youngsters to hunt for the eggs. When a child finds an egg, he matches its letter to a letter on the alphabet strip. You'll know for sure when all 26 eggs have been found!

Kaylene Killebrew, Tuscola, IL

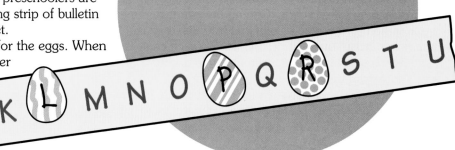

Ant Invaders
Recognizing letters

To prepare for this alphabet game, make a class supply of ant cutouts and label each one with a different letter. Spread a tablecloth on your floor and then scatter the ants on the cloth. To begin, explain that you want to have a picnic but all of these ants have invaded the area. Encourage a child to find an ant labeled with a specific letter and then give it to you. Repeat the process with each remaining child until all the ants have been removed. Then bring out a simple snack for everyone to enjoy— picnic-style!

Erica Crowder
Laurelville Head Start
Laurelville, OH

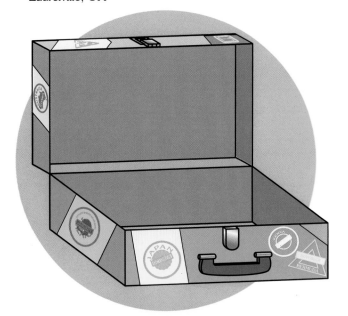

Going on Vacation
Speaking

What would your little ones pack if they were going on a trip? Find out with this catchy rhyme and activity. Gather youngsters around an empty suitcase. After leading them in reciting the rhyme below, invite a child to name an item she would pack. Have her pretend to place the item in the suitcase. Then repeat the process several times, calling on a different child each time.

We're going on vacation to a far-off place.
What should we pack in our big suitcase?

Beth Mickle
First United Methodist Preschool
New Castle, PA

Getting Closer...
Reinforcing letter sounds

Your little ones will love this active game that reinforces letter sounds. Have a volunteer close his eyes while another youngster hides an object, such as a stuffed bear. Have the child open his eyes and then slowly search for the object. As he searches, encourage little ones to repeat the beginning sound of the item's name, saying it quietly when the child is far away from the object and increasing in loudness as he moves closer. Congratulate the child when he finds the item. Then play another round of the game, choosing new volunteers and hiding a different object.

Stephanie Schmidt
Lester B. Pearson Public School
Waterloo, Ontario, Canada

Nursery Rhyme Grab Bag
Reciting nursery rhymes

Youngsters use a bag of props to help them choose nursery rhymes. In advance, gather a collection of small items, such as those listed below, that represent various nursery rhymes. Then place the items in a bag. Have a child reach in the bag and pull out an item. If desired, encourage students to guess what rhyme the item represents. Then help students recite the rhyme. Continue in the same way, having different youngsters remove items from the bag.

> **Suggested rhymes and items:**
> "Humpty Dumpty"—plastic egg
> "Jack, Be Nimble"—candle
> "Little Boy Blue"—horn cutout
> "Mary Had a Little Lamb"—lamb stuffed animal
> "Hickory, Dickory, Dock"—small clock
> "Three Little Kittens"—mitten
> "Little Miss Muffet"—plastic spider

Erica Glass-Terhune
Salem Lutheran Preschool and Child Care Center
Springville, NY

Scoop After Scoop
Following directions

Youngsters listen to descriptions of ice-cream scoops to build a giant ice-cream cone! Make a large ice-cream cone cutout and several colorful scoop cutouts. If desired, draw sprinkles on some of the scoops. Then spread out the cone and scoops on your floor. Gather youngsters around the cutouts. Then give a clue such as "I want one strawberry scoop with chocolate sprinkles" or "I want a scoop that's the same color as Anna's shoes." Invite a child to find the correct scoop and then place it above the cone. Continue in the same way with the remaining scoops to build a giant ice-cream cone.

Mary Jane Spice
Children First Center
Auburn, IN

KIDS IN THE KITCHEN

KIDS IN THE KITCHEN

Put on your apron and step into the kitchen—with your kids, of course! What's on the menu? A generous portion of learning opportunities served up with a batch of fun. Savor the following hands-on activities, perfectly measured for preschool success and teacher ease. Learning has never been so delicious!

Here's what to do:
- Collect the necessary ingredients and utensils using the lists on one of the recipe cards below.
- Follow the teacher preparation guidelines for that activity.
- Photocopy the step-by-step recipe cards on page 39 or 40.
- Color the cards; then cut them out.
- Display the cards on a bulletin board or chart in your snack area so that students can see the title card and directions for the recipe you've selected.
- Discuss the directions with a small group of children.
- Have the children wash their hands; then let the fun begin!

Firefighter's Ladder

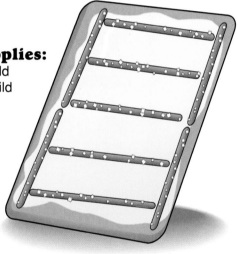

Ingredients for one:
graham cracker (four sections)
frosting
9 pretzel sticks

Utensils and supplies:
paper plate for each child
plastic knife for each child

Teacher preparation:
Arrange the ingredients, utensils, and supplies near the step-by-step recipe cards (page 39).

Jana Sanderson—PreK
Rainbow School
Stockton, CA

Cheesy Spiderweb

Ingredients for one:
string cheese stick
½ green grape
8 pretzel stick halves

Utensils and supplies:
black paper plate for each child

Teacher preparation:
- Cut grapes in half.
- Break pretzel sticks into halves.
- Arrange the ingredients, utensils, and supplies near the step-by-step recipe cards (page 40).

Ada Goren
Winston-Salem, NC

Firefighter's Ladder

Spread. 2

Put. 1

Eat! 5

Add 5. 4

Put 4. 3

The Best of The Mailbox® Preschool • ©The Mailbox® Books • TEC61166

Recipe Cards
Use with "Cheesy Spiderweb" on page 38.

Cheesy Spiderweb

1. Pull.

2. Put.

3. Add 1.

4. Add 8.

5. Eat!

The Best of The Mailbox® Preschool • ©The Mailbox® Books • TEC61166

KIDS IN THE KITCHEN

Put on your apron and step into the kitchen—with your kids, of course! What's on the menu? A generous portion of learning opportunities served up with a batch of fun. Savor the following hands-on activities, perfectly measured for pre-school success and teacher ease. Learning has never been so delicious!

Here's what to do:
- Collect the necessary ingredients and utensils using the lists on one of the recipe cards below.
- Follow the teacher preparation guidelines for that activity.
- Photocopy the step-by-step recipe cards on page 42 or 43.
- Color the cards; then cut them out.
- Display the cards on a bulletin board or chart in your snack area so that students can see the title card and directions for the recipe you've selected.
- Discuss the directions with a small group of children.
- Have the children wash their hands; then let the fun begin!

Santa Mix

Ingredients for one:
M&M's Minis candies (elf noses)
small pretzels (reindeer antlers)
Kix cereal (Santa's buttons)
o-shaped cereal (reindeer food)

Utensils and supplies:
bowl for each ingredient
tablespoon for each ingredient
paper cup for each child

Teacher preparation:
- Pour each ingredient into a separate bowl and add a spoon.
- Arrange the ingredients, utensils, and supplies near the step-by-step recipe cards (see page 42).

Anne Arceneaux
Ward School
Jennings, LA

Bagel Snowman

Ingredients for one:
mini bagel
cream cheese
Cheez Doodles snack
2 pretzel sticks
2 mini chocolate chips

Utensils and supplies:
plastic knife for each child
paper plate for each child

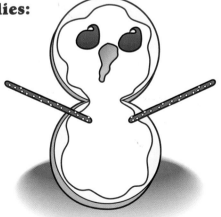

Teacher preparation:
- Slice bagels.
- Arrange the ingredients, utensils, and supplies near the step-by-step recipe cards (see page 43).

Lola Anderson
Canby Head Start
Canby, MN

Recipe Cards

Use with "Santa Mix" on page 41.

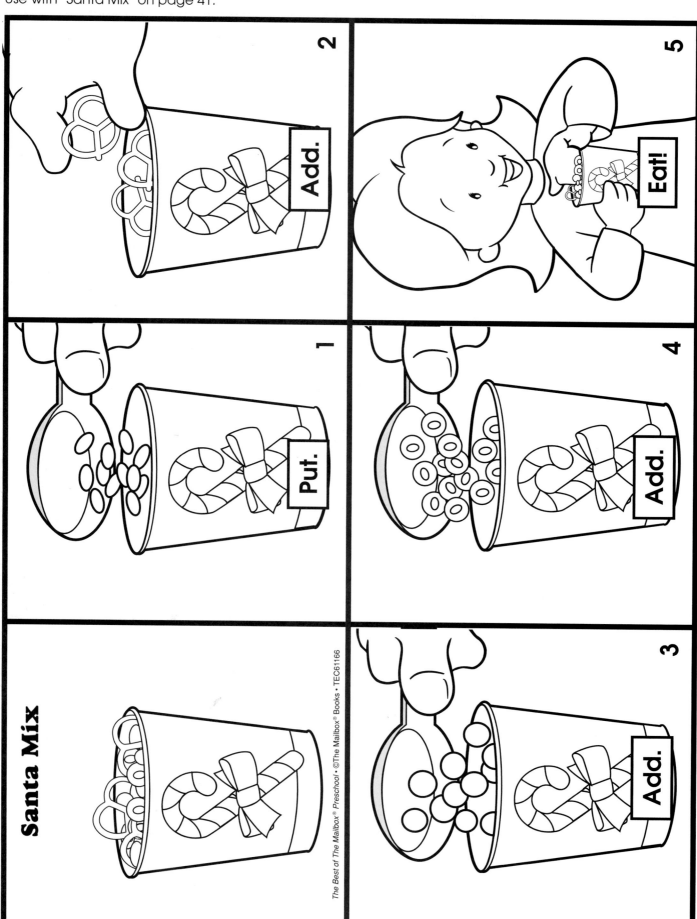

Santa Mix

Put.

Add.

Add.

Add.

Eat!

1

2

3

4

5

The Best of The Mailbox® Preschool • ©The Mailbox® Books • TEC61166

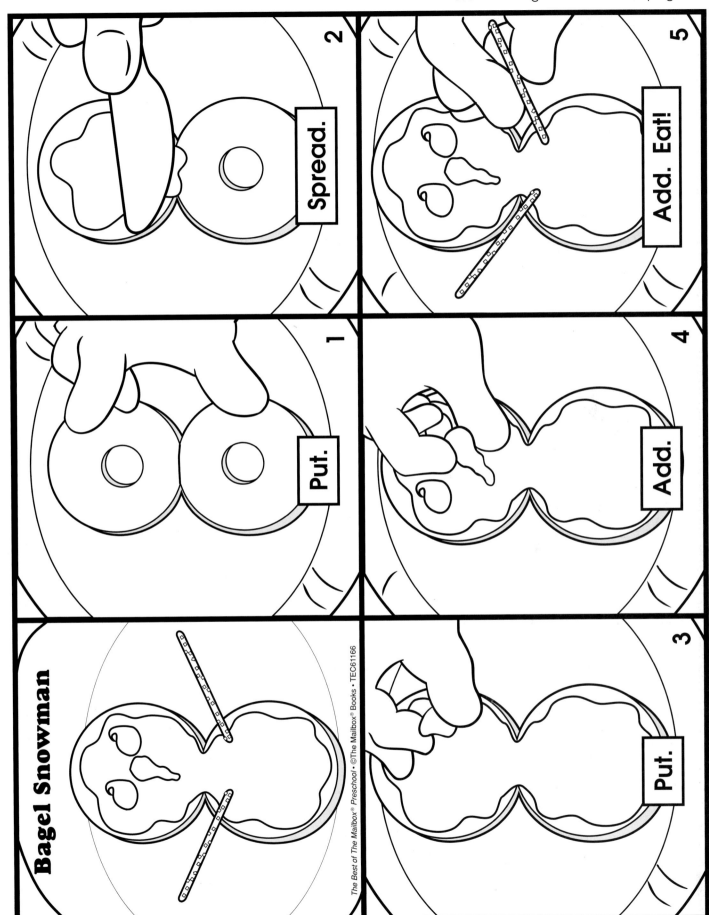

Bagel Snowman

1 — Put.

2 — Spread.

3 — Put.

4 — Add.

5 — Add. Eat!

KIDS IN THE KITCHEN

Put on your apron and step into the kitchen—with your kids, of course! What's on the menu? A generous portion of learning opportunities served up with a batch of fun. Savor the following hands-on activities, perfectly measured for preschool success and teacher ease. Learning has never been so delicious!

Here's what to do:

- Collect the necessary ingredients and utensils using the lists on one of the recipe cards below.
- Follow the teacher preparation guidelines for that activity.
- Photocopy the step-by-step recipe cards on page 45 or 46.
- Color the cards; then cut them out.
- Display the cards on a bulletin board or chart in your snack area so that students can see the title card and directions for the recipe you've selected.
- Discuss the directions with a small group of children.
- Have the children wash their hands; then let the fun begin!

Groundhog Grub

Ingredients for one:
banana half
3 mini chocolate chips (eyes and nose)
2 almond slices (ears)

Utensils and supplies:
3 oz. Dixie cup for each child
(garden scene on the side)

Teacher preparation:
- Cut bananas in half.
- Pour each ingredient into a separate bowl and add a spoon.
- Arrange the ingredients, utensils, and supplies near the step-by-step recipe cards (see page 45).

Itty-Bitty Bunny

Ingredients for one:
pear half
3 M&M's Minis candies (2 eyes and a nose)
2 almond slices (ears)
small marshmallow (tail)

Utensils and supplies:
paper plate for each child

Teacher preparation:
- Drain pear halves.
- Arrange the ingredients, utensils, and supplies near the step-by-step recipe cards (see page 46).

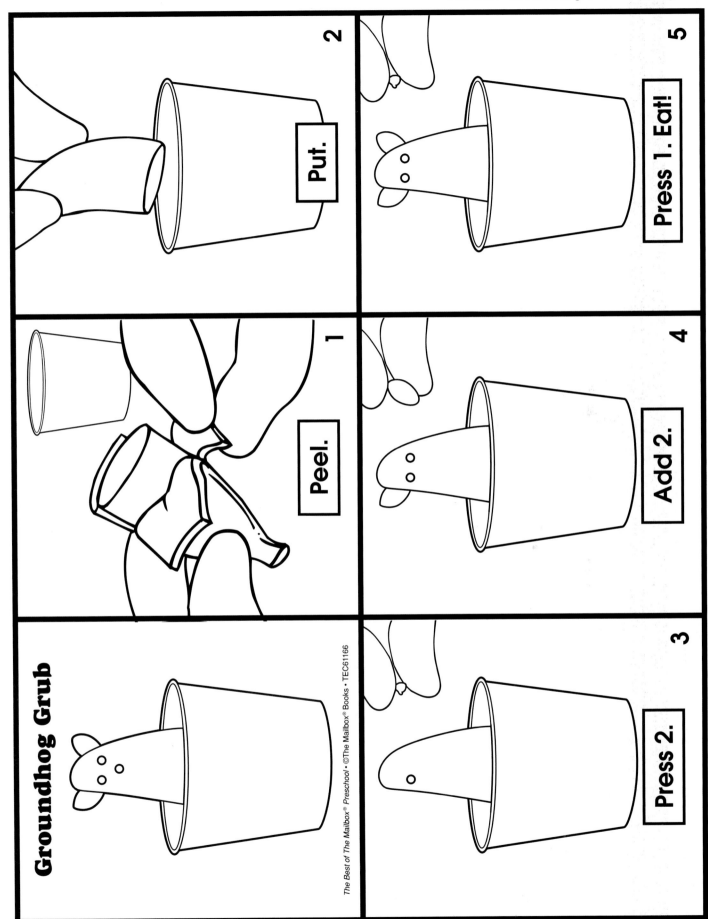

2 Put.

5 Press 1. Eat!

1 Peel.

4 Add 2.

Groundhog Grub

3 Press 2.

The Best of The Mailbox® Preschool • ©The Mailbox® Books • TEC61166

Recipe Cards

Use with "Itty-Bitty Bunny" on page 44.

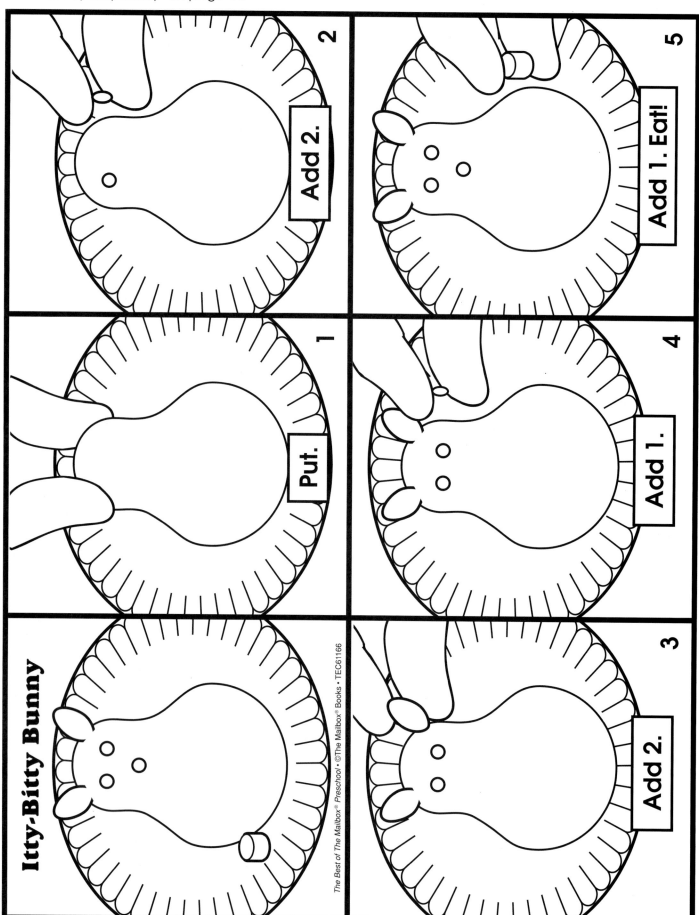

Itty-Bitty Bunny

Put.

Add 2.

Add 2.

Add 1.

Add 1. Eat!

2

1

3

4

5

The Best of The Mailbox® Preschool • ©The Mailbox® Books • TEC61166

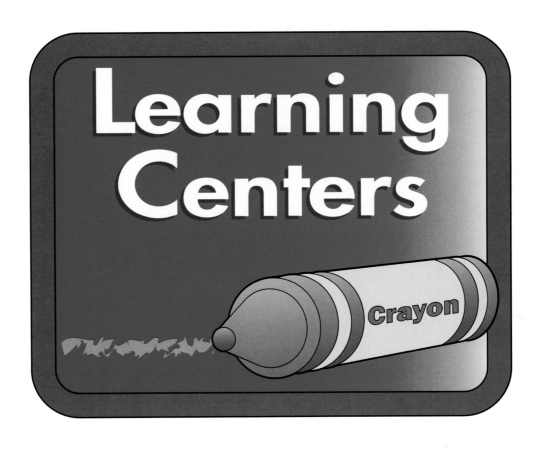

Learning Centers

Simple Stencils
Fine-Motor Area

If you find stencils hard for little hands to manage, try this idea! Trace a large die-cut shape onto the front of a manila folder and then cut out the shape. Place a stack of white paper inside the folder. Close the folder and keep it in your fine-motor area. (Repeat this process to make a supply of folders with various shapes.) A child at this center traces the inside of a cutout shape and then opens the folder and removes her tracing. When she closes the folder again, a fresh sheet of paper is ready for the next student! Invite youngsters to color and cut out their tracings for more fine-motor fun.

Marcia Cochran—Preschool
Kalamazoo Christian West Preschool
Kalamazoo, MI

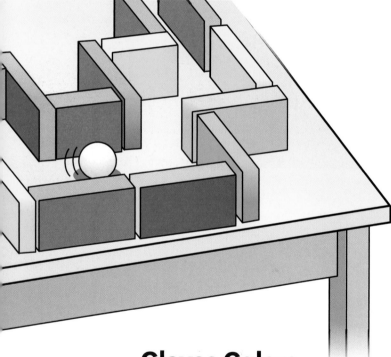

Maze Table
Block Center

Add a table to your block area for this "a-maze-ing" activity! Use wooden blocks to create a twisting pathway along the table, wide enough for a Ping-Pong ball to pass through. Then set a Ping-Pong ball at one end. A child at this center blows through his own individual drinking straw to propel the ball along the path and through the maze. What fun!

Betsy Fuhrmann—PreK
Dodds School
Springfield, IL

Gloves Galore
Sensory Center

Here's a handy way to help youngsters explore their sense of touch! Fill several latex gloves, each with a different substance such as shaving cream, cornmeal, salt, dried beans, popcorn, or cotton. Tie a secure knot in the top of each glove before placing the gloves in your sensory center. Encourage youngsters to touch the gloves and compare their textures and weights. Can anyone guess what's inside each glove?

Tabitha Gay
Ms. Angie's Small World Training Center, Murray, KY

Sharon Jefferies and Susan Tornebene—PreK ESE
Palma Sola Elementary, Bradenton, FL

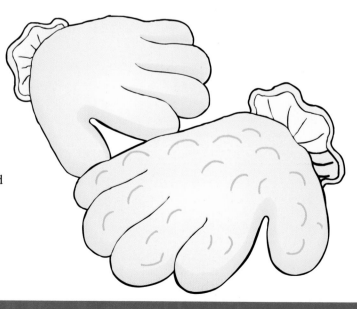

Match Me
Game Center

This fun twist on the traditional game of Memory is personalized for your preschoolers! To make the game, take a head-and-shoulders photo of each child. Have double prints developed. Then mount each photo on a slightly larger tagboard rectangle. Laminate the resulting game cards for durability before placing them in the center. Show students how to use the cards to play a game that challenges a player to find two matching photos of each child. That's a match!

Kate Buschus—Preschool
Lexington, KY

Milk Cap Names
Literacy Center

Use the caps from milk jugs to offer your little ones a serving of print awareness! Personalize a zippered bag for each child. Then write the letters of each child's name on individual milk caps and store the caps inside the corresponding zippered bag. Place children's bags at your literacy center. A child finds her bag and removes the milk caps from it. Then she uses the bag label as a guide as she arranges the lettered milk caps to spell her name. Impressive!

Lisa Terry—Three-Year-Olds
First United Methodist Daycare
Muscle Shoals, AL

Yikes! Spikes!
Math Center

Sorting and counting are "dino-mite" at this math center! Purchase a bag of colorful plastic clothespins. Then, for each color of clothespin, make one copy of the stegosaurus pattern from page 188 on the corresponding color of construction paper. Label each pattern with its color word. Next, laminate the patterns for durability and cut them out. Place the patterns and clothespins at your math center. A child chooses a stegosaurus and clips the same color of clothespins to its back for spikes. When he's added as many spikes as he likes, he counts them. Yikes! That's a lot of spikes!

Kimberly Curry—PreK/Special Education
Cunningham Creek Elementary
Jacksonville, FL

A Little Book of Numbers
Math Center

Combine number identification, counting, fine-motor skills, and bookmaking with this center idea! To prepare, program a booklet page for each numeral from 1 to 10. Add number words if desired. Then copy each page on different colored paper to make a class supply. As you introduce each number, put copies of the corresponding booklet page in your math center, along with a hole puncher. Each child punches a matching number of holes in a page. Compile each child's pages into a minibooklet with a cover that reads "My Little Book of Numbers." Then send the booklets home for youngsters to read and touch!

Sarah Booth—Four- and Five-Year-Olds
Messiah Nursery School
South Williamsport, PA

Autumn Indoors
Sensory Center

Send your preschoolers crunching through leaves—inside! Visit your local craft store and purchase garlands or stems of silk leaves in fall colors. Cut the leaves from the garland and put them in a sensory tub. Add some real pinecones in various sizes. Then invite youngsters to explore! Encourage them to sort the pinecones by size and the leaves by color, size, or shape!

Connie Heintz—PreK
Aldrich Memorial Nursery School
Rochester, MN

Farmer's Market
Dramatic Play

Enhance a harvest theme by inviting your young farmers to pretend they are running a farmer's market in your dramatic-play area. Provide bushel baskets of plastic fruits and vegetables, a balance scale, a toy cash register, shopping baskets, and a supply of paper bags. Add some plaid shirts and bandanas for dress-up, along with empty purses and wallets. Model how to play the parts of the farmer selling her produce and the customer choosing and buying. Then have youngsters start harvesting the fun!

Rhonda Yates—Preschool
Paso Robles, CA

Cool Blocks
Block Center

Brrr! There's a blizzard in your blocks center with this idea! Wrap small, medium, or large cardboard brick blocks or soft blocks in white bulletin board paper. Then encourage youngsters to build snow forts or icebergs for some frosty fun. Encourage snowman building by adding craft foam snowman features backed with Sticky-Tac to the center. Then have preschoolers create snow families among the snow forts. Cool!

Laura Anderson, Partin Elementary
Oviedo, FL

Peppermint Play Dough
Play Dough Center

Add a seasonal scent to your play dough area when you mix up a batch of this dough. Add candy molds, cookie cutters, rolling pins, and four-inch pieces of waxed paper to the center so little ones can wrap up their peppermint creations. To turn your play dough center into a candy cane factory, make two batches of dough—one with and one without food coloring. Show children how to make candy canes by twisting strands of red and white dough together. Now that will create some "excite-mint"!

2 c. flour	2 tbsp. vegetable oil
1 c. salt	4 tsp. cream of tartar
2 c. water	red food coloring
2 tsp. peppermint extract	

Combine all the ingredients in a large pot. Cook over low heat, stirring until dough forms and pulls away from the sides of the pot. Remove the dough from the heat and allow it to cool before using.

Becki Yahm, First Lutheran Children's Programs
Portland, ME

Feed the Penguin
Game Center

Fishing for a fun way to teach color recognition? Try having your preschoolers feed colorful fish to a penguin! Use black and white construction paper to make a penguin on one side of a cardboard box. Make a slit in the box where the penguin's mouth should be; then glue an orange beak above and below the slit. Next, cut out a number of fish from various colors of construction paper. Have pairs of children take turns feeding the fish to the penguin, identifying the color of each one before slipping the fish into its mouth. On another day, label a supply of fish cutouts with shapes, letters, or numbers and encourage youngsters to name them before feeding the penguin. Mmm!

Susan Foulks, University City UMC Weekday School
Charlotte, NC

Brush, Brush, Brush!
Fine-Motor Center

Have little ones brush some less-than-clean teeth in this engaging center. After all, February is Children's Dental Health Month! Laminate large tooth cutouts; then scribble on each one with a dry-erase marker. Place the teeth at a center along with a supply of toothbrushes. A child chooses a tooth and then uses a toothbrush to remove the black marks. Now it's nice and clean!

Brenda Watkins
Sugar Bears
Henderson, NC

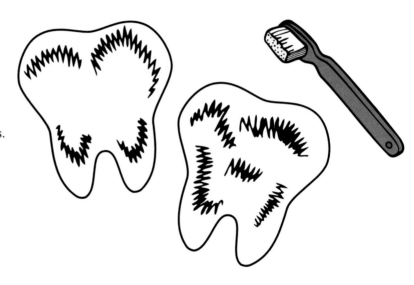

A Sweet Match!
Literacy Center

Label pairs of large colorful heart cutouts with simple matching words, as shown, so they resemble conversation hearts candy. A student chooses a heart, finds the heart with the matching word, and then places the cutouts together. She continues in the same way with each remaining pair.

adapted from an idea by Virginia Sorrells
Peachtree Corners Baptist Preschool
Norcross, GA

St. Patrick's Day Surprise!
Water Table

Everything is green on St. Patrick's Day—even the water in your water table! Use food coloring to whip up a batch of yellow and blue ice cubes. Just before center time, place several ice cubes in your water table. Provide access to mixing spoons. Children can stir the water as the ice cubes dissolve and watch the water change from clear to green. That's so festive!

Casey O'Donnell
Newtonville, MA

Egg Hunt
Sensory Center

How can you provide an exciting egg hunt yet keep it manageable? Use your sensory table! Hide colorful pom-poms (for eggs) among lots of Easter grass. Have youngsters collect the little eggs in small baskets. If you have several different colors of baskets, hide pom-poms in the same colors. Then ask youngsters to sort the eggs by color, matching each one to the same color basket. When the hunt is over, invite the little egg hunters to hide the eggs for another group of friends to find!

Amy Rain Monahan—Three-Year-Olds
Play Pals Program at Saint Anthony's Health Center
Alton, IL

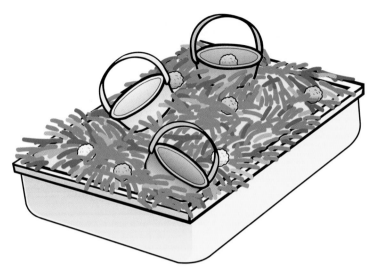

Sarah's Bug

Designer Bugs
Art Center

Creepy-crawly critters are everywhere in springtime, but most likely you've never seen bugs like these! Cut various head, thorax, and abdomen shapes from sponges and prepare each one for stamping. Place the stampers, shallow containers of tempera paint, and white construction paper at the center. Next, help each child mix and match the body parts to sponge-paint a bug of her own design. When the paint is dry, have her use a marker to add legs, antennae, and wings as desired. Then invite her to show her critter to the class and tell a story about it!

Sue Fleischmann—Child and Family Specialist
Waukesha County Project Head Start
Waukesha, WI

Sweet Writing
Writing Center

Fill your classroom with the sweet scent of chocolate, and little ones will instantly be inspired to write! Mix up a batch of chocolate pudding. Then give each child at the center a piece of waxed paper and a spoonful of pudding. Encourage him to spread the pudding over the waxed paper and then use his finger to write letters, numbers, or his name. To erase, he simply spreads the pudding again. Mmm! This writing activity is truly finger-lickin' good!

Brenda Horn—PreK
Livingston Elementary
Livingston, IL

Copy Kids
Writing Center

You can count on little ones being eager to copy words. After all, that's what the big kids do! For an easy-to-manage fine-motor activity, attach the hook sides of six Velcro dots to a poster board chart. Prepare six different word cards, each with a picture clue. Press the loop side of a Velcro dot on the back of each card and then display the cards on the chart. Display the chart within your youngsters' reach. A child removes the card he wants. He copies the word on provided paper and draws his own picture clue. Then he returns the card to the chart. When the little ones ask for new words, simply prepare another set of word cards!

Donna Leonard
Head Start
Dyersville, IA

Counting Candles
Play Dough Center

Everyone loves birthdays! Invite youngsters at your play dough center to create birthday cakes. Then give them a stack of number cards. Have each child take a card and add the corresponding number of birthday candles to her cake. For even more fun, use real birthday cards instead of number cards.

Destiny Simms—Two- and Three-Year-Olds
Kiddie Academy Learning Centers
Laurel, MD

Preschoolers in the Pool
Fine-Motor Area

Preschoolers will love the water in this pool! Set up a child's plastic swimming pool and toss in some blue and green crepe paper streamers and scraps of blue and green construction paper. Add some plastic or vinyl fish that can "swim" in the water. Then put two pairs of scissors in a beach bucket nearby. Encourage pairs of youngsters to sit in the pool and snip away. Remind them not to "splash" the scraps while they practice cutting!

Stephanie Jagoda—PPCD, Rountree Elementary, Allen, TX
Jill Simon—Preschool, Poland Boardman Childcare Center, Poland, OH

Management Tips & Timesavers

Check This Out!

Do your little ones like to borrow books from your classroom to take home? Here's a way to create a simple checkout system. Choose about a dozen books at a time to display in your checkout library. For each one, make a checkout card by cutting out a picture of the book from a book order form. Glue the picture to an index card. Put a small piece of magnetic tape on the back of each card; then display the cards on a magnetic chalkboard. (Use regular tape if your board isn't magnetic.) Display the books or keep them in a special basket nearby. When a child wants to check out a book, write her name in chalk next to the checkout card. When she returns the book, erase her name. Easy! *adapted from an idea by Rivki Silverberg—PreK and K, Head Start, New York City, NY*

Ms. Silverberg

Caitlin

Communication Stickers

Preschool pick-up time can be hectic, and you don't always have a chance to share information about a child's day with his parents. Try this tip to keep in touch! If you need to share information about behavior or boast about a child's great work, jot a few words on a nametag sticker. Then stick the sticker to the child's clothing. Even if you don't get to talk at length with a parent, she can see your note and be sure to ask her child about it. *Mary Gribble—PreK, Country Goose Preschool, River Falls–Prescott, WI*

I shared my blocks today!

Catch a Bubble

If you need youngsters to be quiet for a bit, try softly singing this song together. Then pretend to blow bubbles through a bubble wand, and have each child pretend to do as the song says. Encourage little ones to keep their bubbles in their mouths and not pop them!

(sung to the tune of "Clementine")

Catch a bubble.
Catch a bubble.
Put it right into your mouth!
Catch a bubble.
Catch a bubble.
Put it right into your mouth!

Jennifer Corkern—Preschool, Hobe Sound Child Care Center, Hobe Sound, FL

Cotton Swab Cleanup

Keep your watercolor paint sets neat and tidy with this tip! After a child uses a paint set, run a cotton swab around the ovals of paint to absorb excess paint and water. If paint colors have gotten mixed, dab a swab on top, and it will absorb the mixed color, revealing the original cake of color beneath. *Leslie Campbell—PreK 4, Jack and Jill Christian Preschool, Fernandina Beach, FL*

Yoga Transition

If your little ones have trouble with transition times, try some relaxing yoga. Ask students to sit cross-legged on your carpet as you play some soothing music. Give youngsters a few minutes to simply relax and breathe. After all, preschool is hard work, and everyone needs a break! *Linda Haustein—PreK, George Washington School #1, Elizabeth, NJ*

Binder Clip Tip

Here's an easy way to store sentence strips or bulletin board borders. Clip each set of borders or sentence strips (such as the strips used for a poem or pocket-chart activity) together in a binder clip. Then simply hang each clip on a hook on the wall! *Heather Armstrong, Kathy Dunn Cultural Center, Hasbrouck Heights, NJ*

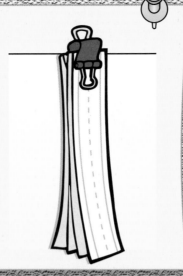

Blow a Kiss

If your circle time is sometimes interrupted with minor complaints, such as "He bumped my knee" or "She sat on my fingers," here's a sweet and easy solution. Say, "Here's a long-distance kiss," and blow a kiss the child's way. Then carry on with your lesson or story. *Harriet Velevis, JCC Preschool, Dallas, TX*

snack time

Preschoolers on Posters

Cue your youngsters about the various parts of the school day with some posters that are sure to get their attention! Take photos of your children washing their hands, cleaning up toys, having a snack, or lining up. Have the photos developed and enlarged to poster-size at a local print shop. Add captions if desired. Then laminate the posters and post them in your classroom. Your little ones will love seeing themselves when you point to a poster to remind them what to do next!

The Passing Song

Use this song to help each youngster take a turn looking at a show-and-tell item or any item you wish to pass around for the group to see.

(sung to the tune of "Mary Had a Little Lamb")

[Child's name] has the [teddy bear, teddy bear, teddy bear].
[Child's name] has the [teddy bear] and wants to pass it on.

Rita Beiswenger, Crescent Avenue Weekday School, Fort Wayne, IN

In and Out Cans

Reinforce name recognition and taking turns with this idea! Decorate two cans and label one "In" and the other "Out." Then write each child's name on a seasonal cutout. Place all the cutouts in the "In" can. When you need a helper, randomly pull out a cutout and show it to your group. Once the task is completed, put the name into the "Out" can. Your preschoolers will soon understand that each child will eventually get a turn to be a helper, and they'll be learning classmates' names too! *Mary Schumacher, Strongsville CoOp Preschool, Strongsville, OH*

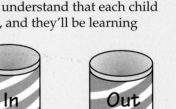

Yarn Cans

Here's a great tip for storing yarn! Put each separate color of yarn ball into a clear tennis ball can. Punch a hole in the plastic lid of the can and thread one end of the yarn through the hole. Your students can easily pull out just as much yarn as they need, and you can easily see when you're almost out of a particular color. You can store several cans in a divided box (check your local grocery store for boxes that hold wine bottles). *Mary Lyons, Oakwood-Windsor Elementary, Aiken, SC*

Alphabet Roundup

Want to signal your little ones that cleanup time is ending? Start saying the alphabet. Explain that by the time you reach z, they should be done cleaning and should be sitting with you in the group area. They'll get the hang of this letter routine in no time! *Stephanie Schmidt, Lester B. Pearson Public School, Waterloo, Ontario, Canada*

UFO Box

Do you and your youngsters sometimes come across stray objects during cleanup time? If you can't remember on the spot where an item or puzzle piece belongs, put it into a box for UFOs, or unidentified found objects. Occasionally go through the box after school and try to put all the items and pieces back where they belong. *Dot Stein, Christian Beginnings Preschool, Prince Frederick, MD*

Outdoor Painting Time

Painting outdoors is great fun in the warm weather! To make management simple, bring along some clothespins, a towel, and a wagon with two buckets, one filled with soapy water and one with clean water. When youngsters finish painting, clip their artwork to a chain-link fence to dry. When it's time to head inside, have little ones wash and rinse their hands in the buckets of water and then dry them on a towel. *Sarah Booth, Messiah Nursery School, South Williamsport, PA*

Double-Duty Dishwasher

Use the dishwasher to wash food—the play food from your dramatic-play area, that is! Put small plastic and vinyl items from your housekeeping area into a fine-mesh laundry bag. Then place the bag on the top rack of your dishwasher. Stop the dishwasher before the drying cycle, and lay out the items on a clean towel to air-dry. *Sheila Shank, St. Paul's Hilltop Christian Nursery School, Torrington, CT*

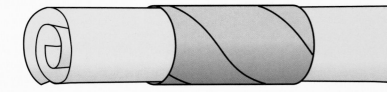

Totally Tubular

Cardboard tubes make handy holders for youngsters' artwork. Simply roll up the artwork, slip it in a tube, and send it home with the youngster. The artwork stays nice and neat so it can be admired at home! *Marisol Rodriguez, Little Learners, Hammond, IN*

Glue on a Stick

Here's an easy method for using white glue with your little ones. Pour a small amount of glue on a paper plate. Then have each child use a craft stick to scoop up the glue and place it on her project! *Trystahjill Harns, Lakeside Christian School, East Lansing, MI*

Simple Flannelboard Cutouts

For quick and easy flannelboard cutouts, simply place felt in your die-cut machine and punch out pieces just as you would when using paper. What a simple way to make props for youngsters' favorite songs and stories! *Michele Barry, USD 506 Mound Valley Grade School, Mound Valley, KS*

Personal Plates

How can youngsters keep track of small pieces needed for projects? They simply place them on personalized plates! Then, when the child is finished with the project, he can place it on top of the plate and you automatically know who the project belongs to! *Sharon A. Beintema, St. John Vianney Preschool, Wyoming, MI*

Soothing Music

While students work on an art project, play a recording of classical music by a well-known composer. Encourage youngsters to talk quietly while the music is playing. After several art experiences, your youngsters just might begin requesting favorite composers! *Dorothy Hsu, Grace Brethren Preschool, Westerville, OH*

PRESCHOOL

On the Level

To place letters in a straight line on your bulletin board, measure down from the top of the board to the level where you want the lettering to begin. Make a mark on the board. Then repeat the process to show approximately where you want the lettering to end. Tack a length of elastic from the first mark to the second. Then use the elastic as a guide for placing your lettering. When you're finished, just remove the elastic and tacks. *Louise Younger, Wee Friends Preschool, Hays, KS*

Lips and Hips

This rhyming reminder helps little ones remember to be quiet and listen. Simply say, "Lips and hips," and have each youngster put one hand on her hips and the pointer finger of her other hand against her lips. This gives little hands something to do while they're waiting for directions. *Sara Doty, Brockport Child Care Center, Brockport, NY*

Cups for Cuttings

Give each child a clean cake frosting container (or other flat-bottomed container) when it's time for cut-and-paste projects. The child cuts out the necessary pieces and then places them in her container for safekeeping until it's time to glue them down. *Susan LaBrie, New Life Christian Preschool, Maple Valley, WA*

All Hands to the Sink!

When youngsters are completing a project that involves making handprints, set up your art station near your classroom sink. Then students can make prints and wash up afterward all in one location! *Karen Cummins, Catholic Social Services of Monroe/Head Start, Temperance, MI*

Title Page Tip

To remember which classroom books have coordinating activities in your files, label the title pages with star stickers. When you open the book you'll be reminded right away to check your files for engaging activities. *Kara Coffman, Newfield Elementary, Newfield, NY*

Our Readers Write

Our Readers Write

Call Ahead

A quick phone call made to each child before the first day of school does wonders for easing back-to-school worries. During your brief conversation tell the child how excited you are to have him in your class. Also tell him what you'll be wearing when he sees you for the first time, so he can spot you right away. This is sure to be a phone call your preschoolers won't forget!

Sara Hicks—PreK, Maple Street PreK, Carrollton, GA

Parent Survival Kit

As parents leave their little ones at school on that first day, hand each one a sweet parting gift. To make each gift, label a small paper bag "Survival Kit." Inside the bag put some Hershey's Hugs and Kisses candies along with a small travel pack of tissues. Your thoughtful gesture is sure to be received with a smile!

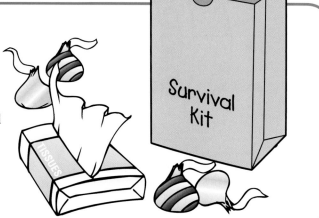

Dellann Frost—Three- and Four-Year-Olds, Litchfield Little School Litchfield, NH

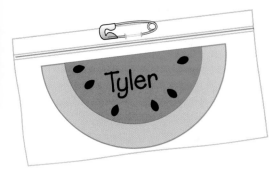

Bag Tags

If you're tired of nametags that rip and tear, try this inexpensive idea! For each child, personalize a cutout that fits inside a snack-size zippered plastic bag. Then seal the cutout inside the bag. Safety-pin each child's bag tag to his clothing, inserting the pin through the thick part of the bag seal. Finally—nametags that last!

Linda Cunningham—PreK, Millard Hawk Elementary School, Central Square, NY

Birthday Wear

Here's a fun way for preschoolers to send happy birthday wishes to a classmate! Cut a length of solid-colored bulletin board border to fit around the birthday child's head. On the border write "Happy Birthday, [child's name]!" Next, ask each classmate to select a sticker (from a supply you've provided) and attach it to the project. When the stickers are in place, staple the ends of the border together. Invite the birthday child to wear her special crown all day! Make plans to design birthday wear for all your students—even those who have birthdays during the summer months.

Dolores Hernandez—Preschool, Children's World, Lubbock, TX

Fridge Clip

Help your preschoolers make these easy-to-use clips for displaying their work on the fridge at home. To make one, hot-glue four wooden clothespins to a wooden paint stick as shown. Have a child paint the stick and clothespins with bright colors. When the paint is dry, use a permanent marker to personalize the stick. Hot-glue heavy duty magnets to the back of the paint stick to complete the project. Send the finished clips home to proudly display preschool work!

Sandi George, Clifton Heights, PA

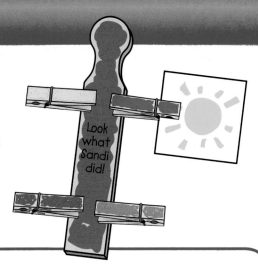

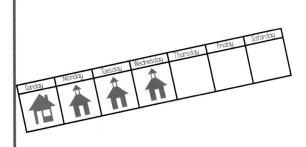

Home Day, School Day

Improve your students' understanding of the calendar by designating which days are home days and which are school days. Use a die-cut of a house or a school to mark each day on the calendar for the month. Let's see…is tomorrow a home day or a school day?

Alison D. Brotschol—PreK, Lexington School–Universal PreK
Jackson Heights, NY

Birthday Books

Make birthdays special with a gift from your Birthday Box! Wrap a medium-size cardboard box in birthday-themed wrapping paper. Then fill it with a supply of paperback books. (This is a great use for your book club bonus points!) On each child's birthday, invite her to open the box and choose a book. Inscribe the inside front cover with the date, the occasion, and your name. What a wonderful way to encourage reading!

Brandee Orgeron—Four- and Five-Year-Olds, Noah's Day Care, Tucson, AZ

Field Trip Shirts

These shirts are convenient for field trips, and they provide a fun record of all the places your youngsters have visited throughout the year! Begin by having each child bring in an oversize white T-shirt. Label the tag in each shirt with a different child's name. Use a fabric marker to print your school name and phone number on the upper left chest area. After each field trip, slip a shirt over a sheet of cardboard. Invite a child to use a related sponge shape to make a fabric-paint print on the shirt. For example, you might use a pumpkin sponge for a trip to a pumpkin patch. When the image is dry, use a fabric marker to write the name of the place visited and the date of the trip. Then write a quote from the child about the trip. What fun to look back later and see what each child thought about your preschool adventures!

Laura Cyborski—Preschool, Southridge Elementary, Highland, IN

Holiday Crayons

I make art time special with crayons in holiday-related shapes! I remove the wrappers from old crayons and place them in a disposable aluminum pan. Then I heat the pan in a 250 degree oven. When the crayons are melted, I remove the pan from the oven and pour the wax into holiday candy molds. When the wax is hard, I simply pop out the shapes!

Janet Knox, Preschool Pals, Crown Point, IN

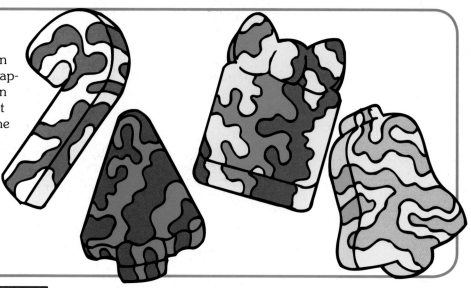

Easy Name Labels

For easy labeling of art projects and other student work, I personalize each pocket in a plastic shoe organizer with a different child's name and picture. Then I place a supply of name slips in each corresponding pocket. A child simply removes a slip and tapes it to her project!

Marsha Feffer, Bentley School—Salem Early Childhood Center, Salem, MA

Who Pudding

As a follow-up to a reading of Dr. Seuss' story *How the Grinch Stole Christmas!* I have youngsters make Who Pudding! I add the pudding mix and milk to a bowl according to package directions. My students take turns stirring the mixture until the pudding is thick. Then each child adds a sprinkle of special Who Seasonings (colored sprinkles). They enjoy their snack as we revisit the story!

Melissa Goodrich, Northwest Daycare Center, South Bend, IN

A Gift for Everyone!

Rather than give me personal gifts for the holidays, I request that parents send a gift that can be used by the entire class, such as a book or stickers. My students and I are so excited to unwrap and use these special gifts!

Heidi Peck, First United Methodist Preschool and Daycare, Cedartown, GA

Snowman in the Classroom!

My little ones have a lot of frosty fun with this little snowman! I fill a small, a medium, and a large balloon with water; then I place them in the freezer. When the water is frozen, I remove the balloons and use a sprinkling of salt to fuse the balls together to resemble a snowman. I use cotton batting to prop up the snowman in a plastic container. Students dress him up with felt scraps and old accessories until he melts away!

Jennifer Avegno, Carousel Preschool, Cypress, CA

Snacktime Manners

Each day during snacktime, I ask each child whether he would like to have a serving of the particular snack for the day. He responds by saying, "No, thank you" or "Yes, please." When children are comfortable answering the question, I throw in some questions guaranteed to produce giggles, such as "Would you like some purple pizza?" or "Would you like to have some dinosaur stew?" Little ones love the silly questions and continue to practice using polite words!

Linda Ludlow, Bethesda Christian Schools, Brownsburg, IN

Donation Tree

I let my preschoolers' parents know what's needed for upcoming projects with a donation tree! I label each of several index cards with items I need and the date they're needed by. I insert each one into a photo tree and then display the tree in the classroom. A parent can remove a card and then bring in the item by the designated date.

Heather Parker, Our Guardian Angel Home Daycare, Monroe, MI

Paint Pops

To make paint pops, I squirt tempera paint into the sections of an ice cube tray. Then I cover the tray with aluminum foil and poke a craft stick through the foil and into each cup. After the paint pops freeze, I remove them from the tray and my little ones use them to paint. The colors are bright and oh so cool!

Svetlana Borukhova, Herbert G. Birch Western Queens ECC, New York City, NY

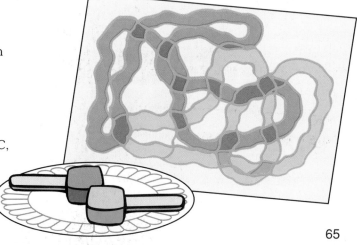

Class Book Covers

Gift bags make great covers for class books! I trim off the bottom and one side of a gift bag. After I fold in the remaining side, I reinforce it with tape. Then I label the front of the bag with the title of the class book. Finally, I use brads to attach the completed pages to the reinforced strip. The bag's handles make this class book easy to display and store!

Judy Knapp, Wilcox Primary, Twinsburg, OH

Weather Photos

I cut photographs from nature magazines that show various types of weather. Then I post the photos in our daily weather center and label each one. Weather seems very real to my youngsters when they view it this way. I've also labeled pictures of the seasons and added them to this display!

Sherrie Kautman, Handicare Inc., Coralville, IA

Brilliant Pasta

To dye pasta bright, beautiful colors, I use acrylic paint from the craft store! I squeeze about one-third of a small bottle of paint into a large resealable plastic bag. Then I pour in a supply of pasta. I squeeze and shake the bag until the paint coats all the pasta. Then I pour the pasta onto newspapers to dry. After a few minutes of drying time, I rub the pasta between my hands to make sure there aren't any pieces stuck together. This method works with regular acrylic paint as well as metallic, glitter, and neon varieties!

Jean Blosser, Joy Early Childhood Education Center, Glendale, AZ

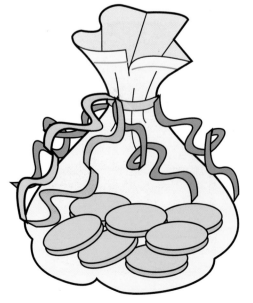

Pot-o'-Gold Hunt

We celebrate St. Patrick's Day with a treasure hunt! For each child, I place a few chocolate coins in a small resealable plastic bag and then tie curling ribbon around the bag, as shown. Then I hide the resulting gold around the classroom. My little ones love to search the room and find their pieces of leprechaun gold!

Tammy LaMothe-Toland, Suffolk, VA

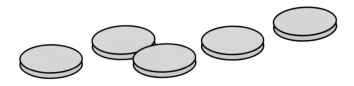

Special Seeds

To make this Mother's Day gift, I cut a supply of sealed business envelopes in half. Each child stamps decorations on his envelope half. Then he slips a package of seeds in the envelope and glues the poem shown to the front. I punch two holes in the envelope as shown; then I thread a ribbon through the holes and tie a bow. This adorable gift has always been a big hit!

Sharon Winter, Our Lady of Hope/St. Luke School, Baltimore, MD

These little seeds of love will grow

Stronger every day, you know.

So plant them in the ground this May.

And have a happy Mother's Day!

Individual Flannelboards

My youngsters had difficulty sharing the limited amount of space on our flannelboard. To solve this problem, I cut pieces of felt to fit in large box lids. I glued the felt in place and voilà! We had several personal, portable flannelboards!

Nan La Fitte, Wesley Academy, Houston, TX

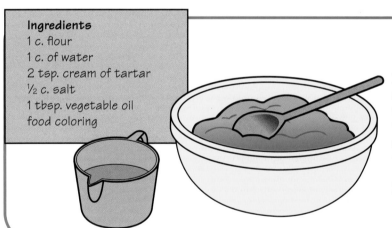

Ingredients
1 c. flour
1 c. of water
2 tsp. cream of tartar
½ c. salt
1 tbsp. vegetable oil
food coloring

Microwave Play Dough

I make all of my play dough in the microwave! Mix in a microwave-safe bowl the ingredients shown. Place the bowl in the microwave and cook the ingredients on high for three minutes, stopping to stir after each minute. Then turn the dough onto a floured surface and knead it until it's cool. Store the play dough in an airtight container.

Daisy Green, The Learning Center, Hagerstown, MD

An Artsy Display

For our student art show, I transform cardboard boxes into unique displays. I collect a variety of large cardboard boxes and then paint them black. Next, I stack the boxes at different angles, as shown, and attach student artwork to the sides. After the art show, it's easy to break down the boxes and store them for next year!

Jacqueline A. Higgins, Eastminster Presbyterian Pre-School, Indialantic, FL

Father's Day Booklets

To make a booklet cover, I cut two horizontal slits in a sheet of paper and then fold the strips at an angle to resemble a shirt collar as shown. I have each youngster decorate a pocket cutout and a preprogrammed tie cutout. Then I help him glue the cutouts to the shirt and glue the collar over the tie. Then I staple each cover to two sheets of paper labeled as shown. Youngsters dictate a response on the second page and then add drawings to both pages.

Karen Eiben, The Learning House Preschool
La Salle, IL

Love, Justin

Happy Father's Day!

My daddy is special because <u>he always gives me hugs.</u>

This is my daddy!

Memory Puzzles

Near the end of the school year, I enlarge photos I've taken of class events, such as field trips or parties. I glue the photos to tagboard and then puzzle-cut each photo and place it in a separate resealable bag. My students love assembling the pictures and reviewing the fun things we did throughout the year.

Beth Baranowski, Roselle Park, NJ

That Was Fun!

To help little ones leave for the summer with fond memories of preschool, we spend the last week of school repeating activities that students have particularly enjoyed. My youngsters suggest stories they want to hear, games they want to play, and the toys and activities they want in the centers. What a fun and memorable week!

Susan Riehl, Ross Preschool, Port Huron, MI

Beginner Basketball

Even my littlest preschoolers can handle this basketball hoop! I place a small swimming pool hoop in our outdoor play area and provide access to a variety of foam balls. It's easy for my youngsters to make a basket and retrieve the ball afterward.

Karen Eiben

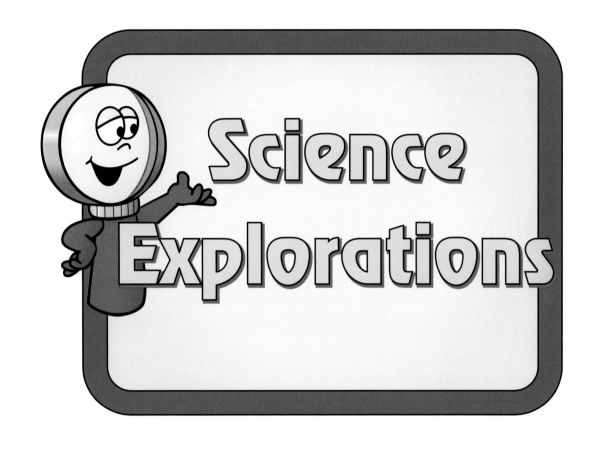

Science

Skin—the Great Protector

Little ones learn what an important purpose our skin serves with this demonstration.

Invite a small group to join you at a table. Have each youngster look at the skin of her arm and talk about its importance.

Cover the bowl of water with plastic wrap to simulate skin, and use a rubber band to secure it in place. Explain to students that the plastic wrap is like our skin because it protects the water in the bowl as our skin protects the inside of our bodies.

To demonstrate a cut, use a rock to make a small hole in the plastic-wrap skin. Ask students what they do when they get boo-boos. Have a child wipe the cut with a towel, and instruct another youngster to place a bandage over it.

Repeat Step 3 to show that our skin and a bandage can help keep germs and dirt out of our bodies. After wiping away the dirt, have youngsters check the water in the bowl for dirt particles.

Explorations

To demonstrate the purpose of our skin, you will need the following:

bowl with water   damp towel
plastic wrap   rock
large rubber band   bandage
dirt

STEP 3

Have a student put some dirt on the plastic-wrap skin. Did the skin protect the water inside? You bet!

STEP 4

Invite another child to use a damp towel to gently wipe the dirt away, simulating washing dirty skin.

Did You Know?

Check out the thickness of a sheet of paper. The outermost layer of our skin is about that thick over most of the body.

What Now?

Rewrap the bowl with plastic wrap and secure it with a rubber band. Invite youngsters to test the plastic-wrap skin with paint or markers. Is it paintproof and markerproof? Yes!

Science

Huff and Puff!

Little ones have a grand time huffing and puffing during this exploration of air!

by Lucia Kemp Henry

STEP 1

Ask a small group of students to sit along one side of a table. Give each child a plastic drinking straw and a craft feather.

STEP 2

Ask each child to move her feather across the table by blowing air through her straw. Ask students why the feathers can be moved in this way. Help them conclude that a craft feather is light and moves easily.

STEP 5

Have students test their predictions.

STEP 6

Have students sort the test objects into three groups according to which ones are easy to move, which ones are hard to move, and which ones can't be moved.

Explorations

To discover whether items can be moved by a stream of air, each student in a small group needs the following:

plastic drinking straw
craft feather
wooden block (or something of similar weight)
cotton ball
small rock
jumbo paper clip
craft stick

STEP 3

Give each child a wooden block. Challenge him to make the block move by blowing air through his straw. Ask students why the block cannot be moved in this way. Help them conclude that a wooden block is heavy and does not move easily.

STEP 4

Give students the remaining objects. Engage them in predicting whether each object can be moved by blowing air through a straw.

This Is Why

When air is forced through a straw, it moves quickly and has strength. The air has the power to move lightweight objects.

What Now?

Invite students to experiment with different ways to move a test object with air. First, suggest that the child try to move the object by blowing air directly on it. Then challenge her to move the object by blowing air through a clean paper towel tube and/or paper cone. Have the student compare the methods and decide which one works best!

Science

Mixing Up Colors

Little ones whip up secondary colors with this vivid investigation!

by Suzanne Moore, Tucson, AZ

STEP 1

That's blue!

Tint each of three containers of whipped topping a different primary color. Gather a small group of youngsters and present the whipped topping. Encourage students to identify the colors.

STEP 2

?

Place dollops of blue and yellow whipped topping in a bowl. Ask youngsters to predict what will happen when the two colors are mixed.

STEP 5

What will happen?

Repeat Steps 2 and 3 with yellow and red whipped topping and with blue and red whipped topping.

STEP 6

Give each child slices of fruit and dollops of green, purple, and orange whipped topping. Invite each child to dip her fruit into these tasty secondary colors and then nibble on her snack.

Explorations

To explore color mixing, you will need the following:
3 small containers of whipped topping
red, yellow, and blue food coloring (gel food coloring works best)
3 bowls
3 spoons
a small paper plate for each child
fruit slices for each child

STEP 3

Invite a child to stir the whipped topping as the remaining youngsters observe.

STEP 4

It's green!

When the colors are completely mixed, encourage children to identify the new secondary color.

Did You Know?

Some animals can't see certain colors. In fact, it's thought that dogs see the world in shades of just one color!

What Now?

Experiment with some chilly color mixing! Place water in the sections of an ice cube tray and then tint the water primary colors (yellow, blue, and red). Have each child choose two cubes in different colors and place them in a glass of clear soda. As the ice melts, the soda transforms into a secondary color!

Name _____

Mixing Up Colors

We mixed ⬡ and ⬡ .

It made ⬡ .

It tasted 🙂 😐 🙁 .

Ask me to tell you more about our science investigation!

The Best of The Mailbox® Preschool • ©The Mailbox® Books • TEC61166

SONGS & SUCH

Handsome Hands

Spotlight successful hand washing with this catchy ditty! Have youngsters pantomime turning on a sink and putting a dollop of soap on their hands; then lead them in performing the song.

(sung to the tune of "Are You Sleeping?")

Tops and bottoms,	*Rub tops and palms of hands.*
Tops and bottoms.	
In between,	*Rub between fingers.*
In between.	
All around your hands,	*Rub all over each hand and wrist.*
All around your hands.	
Now we're clean.	*Hold up hands and wiggle fingers.*
Now we're clean.	

Tina Rumburg
First Presbyterian
Gastonia, NC

The Name Chant

This action-packed chant helps little ones learn the names of their classmates! Begin leading youngsters in the chant, substituting a student's name when indicated. During the first and second lines, invite the student named to join you in performing the action described; then have his classmates join in for the remainder of the chant. Repeat the chant with different student names and actions (see the suggested actions below).

[Austin], [Austin], clap your hands!
[Austin], [Austin], clap your hands!
Everybody clap your hands.
Clap with [Austin]!

Suggested actions: *touch your nose, pat your head, touch your knees, nod your head, stomp your feet, wiggle your hands, turn around*

adapted from an idea by Amy Poole
Jack and Jill Early Learning Center
Norcross, GA

Leafspeak

After teaching this little song, take your youngsters on a walk through some crunchy fall leaves. They'll be asking to sing the song again!

(sung to the tune of "Clementine")

Leaves are falling; leaves are falling
From the trees down to the ground.
Some are orange and some are yellow.
Some are even red and brown!

They are swishing; they are crackling
When I go out for a walk.
They are saying, "It is autumn!"
In their leafy kind of talk!

Days of the Week!

This peppy addition to calendar time is sure to put a spring in your little ones' steps! Have youngsters march in a circle as they recite this version of the days of the week.

There's Sunday and there's Monday.
There's Tuesday and there's Wednesday.
There's Thursday and there's Friday,
And then there's Saturday!
The days of the week. Yahoo!

Suzan Hill—Three-Year-Olds
6th and Izard Day School
Little Rock, AR

Heather McCarthy—Toddlers
Jack N Jill Childcare
Quincy, MA

Big Orange Pumpkins

This little ditty takes pumpkins from seeds to festive jack-o'-lanterns!

(sung to the tune of "The Itsy-Bitsy Spider")

Pumpkins start as fat seeds
Planted in the ground.
Then they push up vines
That wiggle all around.
Soon pumpkins grow.
They're big and orange too.
Then you carve a jack-o'-lantern
That lights up and says, "Boo!"

Deborah Garmon
Groton, CT

Five Little Train Cars

Choo, choo! All aboard this little train rhyme!

Five little train cars all in a row,
The first one said, "Which way will we go?"
The second one said, "Down the track."
The third one just said, "Clickety-clack."
The fourth one said, "We have a job to do."
The fifth one said, "I'm following you."
"Choo, choo," said the engine strong and bright,
And the happy little train chugged out of sight!

Shelley Hoster—PreK
Jack and Jill Early Learning Center
Norcross, GA

Hanukkah Time

Sing this little song to brighten the Hanukkah holiday!

(sung to the tune of "Up on the Housetop")

Menorah in the window shining bright,
Hanukkah time is here tonight.
Time to give and time to share
With friends and family everywhere.
Hanukkah, what a sight!
Hanukkah is here tonight.
Menorah in the window shining bright,
Hanukkah time is here tonight!

Randy McGovern
Twin Oaks Country Day School
Freeport, NY

Trimming the Tree

Have youngsters help decorate your classroom Christmas tree as they sing this song! For additional verses, substitute *shiny stars, candy canes,* and *icicles* for *Christmas lights.*

*(sung to the tune of
"She'll Be Comin' Round the Mountain")*

We'll be trimming our tree with [Christmas lights].
We'll be trimming our tree with [Christmas lights].
We'll be trimming our tree
For the whole wide world to see.
We'll be trimming our tree with [Christmas lights].

LeeAnn Collins
Sunshine House Preschool
Lansing, MI

A Little Valentine

This Valentine's Day ditty is sure to delight your little ones! Lead students in singing the song. After the spoken line, have one of your youngsters name who they would give the valentine to. Repeat the song several times, having a different student answer the question each time.

(sung to the tune of "Baby Bumblebee")

I'm bringing home a little valentine.
It says, "I love you. Please won't you be mine?"
I'm bringing home a little valentine.
Who should I give it to? (spoken)

Karen Amatrudo
The Learning Village
Madison, CT

I love you. Please won't you be mine?

Martin Luther King Jr.

Dr. Martin Luther King Jr. is honored when your students sing this song!

(sung to the tune of "You Are My Sunshine")

You are a hero
To many people.
And of your praises,
We love to sing.
You said we should be
Kind to each other.
Your name is Martin Luther King!

Linda Gordetsky
Palenville, NY

A Bunny Ballad

Little ones quickly guess the popular animal that is the focus of this springtime song!

(sung to the tune of "Do Your Ears Hang Low?")

Do your ears stand high?
Do they point up to the sky?
Do you like to paint your eggs
With some pink and purple dye?
Do you have big feet that hop?
Could you eat a carrot crop?
Do your ears stand high?

Letter and Sound Review

This playful review of a letter's name and sound is sure to become a favorite! To perform the song, provide each child with two stick puppets of the featured letter: one uppercase and one lowercase.

(sung to the tune of "Where Is Thumbkin?")

Where is [B]? Where is [B]?	Hold puppets behind back.
Here I am! Here I am!	Hold up one puppet, then the other.
Can you say the [B] sound?	Wiggle one puppet.
Can you say the [B] sound?	Wiggle the other puppet.
[/b/ /b/ /b/, /b/ /b/ /b/]	Wiggle both puppets.

Catherine Brubaker—Head Start
Branch ISD
Coldwater, MI

Rainbows!

Introduce youngsters to the weather conditions needed to make a rainbow! If desired, make puppets like the one shown for students to use while singing this colorful tune!

(sung to the tune of "I'm a Little Teapot")

I'm a little rain cloud in the sky.	Hold up the rain cloud puppet.
I can help make rainbows if I try.	
I make a little rain in the bright sunshine,	Flip the puppet to show the sun and rain.
And out pops a rainbow. It sure is fine!	Separate the two sticks to show the rainbow.

Kathleen S. Peterson—Speech Associate, Arlington Elementary, Tacoma, WA

A Great Year

This song is a fun way to wrap up the school year! It also makes a nice addition to an end-of-the-year program.

(sung to the tune of "I've Been Working on the Railroad")

I've been having fun in preschool,
Learning all year long.
I can tell you all about it.
Just listen to this song.

We've been learning shapes and colors,
Letters and numbers too.
I've learned how to share with others.
Now our year is through.

Aimee Gross
Living Word Christian Academy
West Haven, CT

Summertime!

Sun, pool parties, and backyard playtime—summertime is one terrific season! Have students celebrate summer with this bouncy little tune.

(sung to the tune of "Jingle Bells")

Summertime, summertime—
It is so much fun!
Playing in our backyard
In the summer sun.
Splash with friends in the pool.
We have such a blast!
It's too bad that summertime
Has to go so fast!

Deborah Garmon
Groton, CT

Storytime

Chrysanthemum

Written and Illustrated by Kevin Henkes

Chrysanthemum, a little mouse, adores her lovely name. But when she goes to school her classmates make fun of her, saying that her name is too long and flowery. Then one day a very special teacher helps the children see that the name Chrysanthemum is absolutely perfect!

ideas contributed by Janet R. Boyce, Cokato, MN

My name is Conner!

Before You Read

Set the stage for this storytime selection with a quick name introduction! To begin, explain to youngsters that names are very special and that each student should be proud of his name. Then say, "My name is [your name]." Encourage students to say hello and then repeat your name. Next, prompt a child to say his name in the same way and encourage students to say hello and repeat the child's name. Continue in the same way for each child in the class. Then explain that the story you're about to read is about a little mouse with a very unique name!

Kara

After You Read

Youngsters are sure to bloom before your eyes with this flowery follow-up! Give each child in a small group a white construction paper circle. Provide access to yellow and orange ink pads. Then have each student make fingerprints on her circle to transform it into a flower. Invite each child to glue her flower to a green construction paper stem. Then have her glue green construction paper leaves to the stem. Explain that the flower resembles a chrysanthemum, the kind of flower that the mouse in the story is named after. Write each child's name on her flower. Then attach it to a bulletin board titled "Absolutely Perfect Names."

Swimmy

Written and Illustrated by Leo Lionni

How will a school of fish frolic in the sea when a big hungry tuna is lurking about? A little fish named Swimmy has the answer! This timeless tale of teamwork will enthrall your youngsters from beginning to end!

Before You Read

Lead into the story with a demonstration of teamwork! Before children arrive for the day, scatter several blocks (or other toys) around the room. To begin, gather youngsters in your large-group area. Begin picking up the blocks; then stop and explain that it will take a long time if you continue by yourself. Invite the students to help you. Once the blocks are back where they belong, explain that when people work together they can often do things faster and more easily than if one person were to try to complete a task by herself. Then tell youngsters that the book you're about to share is about a school of fish that work together so they can swim safely.

After You Read

Remind youngsters of Swimmy's splendid idea with this simple snack! Draw a fish shape on a paper plate for each child. Give each student a plate and have her arrange orange fish-shaped crackers within the fish outline. Encourage her to add a fish-shaped cracker in a different color to make the fish's eye. Then invite her to nibble on her treat. Look—it's Swimmy!

Jana Sanderson
Rainbow School
Stockton, CA

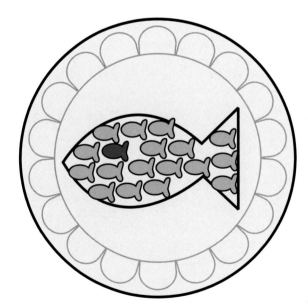

The Night Before Thanksgiving

Written by Natasha Wing
Illustrated by Tammie Lyon

Oh, what a Thanksgiving feast is in store for this extended family! Join in this lighthearted tale as the meal is prepared, the family arrives, and everyone enjoys each other's company—and leftovers the next day!

Before You Read

A huge platter of roast turkey is sure to get youngsters' attention! Cut a large turkey-and-platter shape from tan bulletin board paper and display it in your reading area. Gather students and discuss the upcoming holiday. Encourage each youngster to share a favorite Thanksgiving food or tradition as you record his thoughts on the cutout. When everyone has had a turn, invite students to settle in for the story.

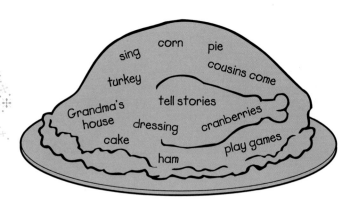

After You Read

Graphing

So which students host Thanksgiving guests? This simple graph makes it easy to find out! Use electrical tape to make a large two-column graph on a vinyl tablecloth; then program sheets of white construction paper as shown. Give each child a small white paper plate and instruct her to write her name on it. Read the question aloud and then invite each child to tape her plate to the appropriate side of the graph. Discuss the graph results as a class. Mount the completed graph on a bulletin board for an eye-catching display.

Corduroy

Written and Illustrated by Don Freeman

Corduroy, a cuddly stuffed bear, sits on a department store shelf day after day hoping someone will take him home. Despite his missing button, a nice little girl decides that he is the bear she's always wanted. Finally, Corduroy has the home—and the friend—he's been longing for!

ideas contributed by Suzanne Moore, Tucson, AZ

Before You Read

Introduce this adorable story with a quick button search! Before youngsters enter the room, place a brightly colored jumbo button within view of your circle-time area. Gather youngsters and tell them that you have lost a button. Describe what it looks like. Then have students scan the room from their seats. When they see the button, retrieve it and congratulate them on their keen observation skills. Then explain that the book selection for storytime is about a teddy bear who also happens to be looking for a button!

Corduroy climbs down!

After You Read

Corduroy climbs *down* from the shelf, he rides *up* the escalator, and he topples *off* the bed! This little bear sure knows his positional words! Have each child transform a bear cutout into a stick puppet similar to the one shown. During a retelling of the story, invite youngsters to use their puppets to imitate the teddy bear's movements.

In the Tall, Tall Grass

Written and Illustrated by Denise Fleming

This colorful book treats students to a caterpillar's-eye view of the critters that live in the tall, tall grass. The rhyming text and vibrant words are used to describe animals like bees, hummingbirds, ants, and bats as they go about their busy day.

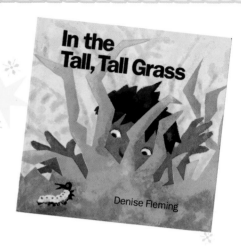

ideas by Lucia Kemp Henry, Fallon, NV

Before You Read

Spark students' curiosity about the animals they'll see in the story with this imaginative idea. To prepare, draw grass shapes on a 9" x 12" sheet of green construction paper, as shown, and cut them out. Glue a jumbo craft stick to the straight edge of the grass. Ask your youngsters to sit in a circle; then show them the cover of the book. Discuss what kinds of animals the child in the illustration might see other than the caterpillar. Then invite each youngster to hold the grass puppet, pretend to look through it, and imagine what kind of animal she would like to discover in the tall, tall grass. Have each child share her selected animal by inserting its name in the chant below. After each student has had a turn, encourage youngsters to listen for their animal pick during the story.

Class: What could [child's name] see in the tall, tall grass?
Child: I could see a [animal's name] in the tall, tall grass!

After You Read

Can your little ones hum, flap, scurry, and snap just like the critters in the tall, tall grass? Try this movement activity to find out. Review the animals in the book and how each one maneuvers; then demonstrate a simple way to mimic each animal's movements. Next, take youngsters to a grassy area outside. Read each line of descriptive text from the book; then invite the group to move around the area just like the critter you've described. Use the movements shown as a guide.

Book Text	Movements
Crunch, munch, caterpillars lunch.	*Pretend to munch.*
Ritch, ratch, moles scratch.	*Scratch the ground.*
Dart, dip, hummingbirds sip.	*Pretend to sip through a straw.*
Skitter, scurry, beetles hurry.	*Crawl quickly.*
Strum, drum, bees hum.	*Buzz.*
Zip, zap, tongues snap.	*Stick out tongue.*
Crack, snap, wings flap.	*Flap arms.*
Hip, hop, ears flop.	*Use hands to show ears flopping while hopping.*
Pull, tug, ants lug.	*Pretend to carry something heavy.*
Stop, go, fireflies glow.	*Flash hands.*
Slip, slide, snakes glide.	*Pretend to slither.*
Lunge, loop, bats swoop.	*Pretend to fly in circles.*

The Little Engine That Could
Written by Watty Piper
Illustrated by George and Doris Hauman

When an engine breaks down on its way to deliver food and toys to the other side of the mountain, a little blue engine helps out and, in the process, demonstrates the power of positive thinking. This uplifting story has long been considered a classic.

ideas contributed by Ada Goren, Winston-Salem, NC

Puff, puff!

Before You Read

Youngsters will be ready to settle in for a train story after some locomotive motion! Have students get in a line. Then lead them around the room, reciting the chant shown several times and encouraging them to move like a train. Finally, have your little ones pull into the station and take a seat for a read-aloud of this fun story.

> The train is going down the track—
> Puff, puff, chug, chug,
> Clickety, clickety, clickety clack.

After You Read

Attach a blue engine cutout to your wall. Then write a simple goal on the engine, such as "We will all line up nicely to go to outdoor playtime." As youngsters are lining up, encourage them to softly chant, "I think I can, I think I can." Then, as students are walking outdoors, give them each a high five and prompt them to say, "I thought I could, I thought I could."

We will all line up nicely to go to outdoor playtime.

Chicka Chicka Boom Boom

Written by Bill Martin Jr. and John Archambault
Illustrated by Lois Ehlert

Skit skat skoodle doot, flip flop flee—you've got to read this book about a coconut tree! A group of mischievous lowercase letters race to the top of a coconut tree. But will there be enough room? This engaging rhythmic adventure is sure to enthrall your little ones.

ideas contributed by Ada Goren, Winston-Salem, NC

Before You Read

Present an adhesive bandage to your youngsters. Ask them to explain what bandages are used for and then share experiences they've had using them. After they share their stories, explain that the book you're about to read has several characters that topple out of a tree and one of them has to use a bandage. Then have little ones listen to a read-aloud of this classic story, encouraging youngsters to watch for the bandage among the pile of letters.

After You Read

Have students sit in a circle on the floor. Review the illustration that shows all the letters in a pile after they've fallen out of the tree. Then place a pile of letter cutouts in the middle of the circle to resemble those in the book. Lead students in reciting the rhyme shown. Then encourage a child to pick up a letter and help him identify its name. Repeat the process several times, reciting the rhyme and calling on a different child each time.

Chicka chicka boom boom
Flip, flop, flee!
What letter fell
From the coconut tree?

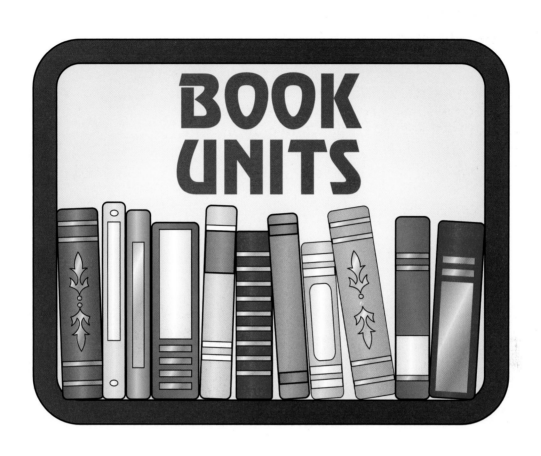

BOOK UNITS

The Kissing Hand

Written by Audrey Penn
Illustrated by Ruth E. Harper and Nancy M. Leak

The Kissing Hand
by AUDREY PENN

Illustrations by Ruth E. Harper and Nancy M. Leak

Child & Family Press

Leaving a loved one can be difficult for a child. It certainly is for the little raccoon named Chester when he has to leave his mother to go to school. But Chester's loving mother gives him a kissing hand so that he will always have her love with him. Going to school doesn't seem as scary now that he has his mother's love right in the palm of his hand.

ideas contributed by Heather Miller—PreK, Creative Playschool, Auburn, IN

A Kiss on the Hand

Making a prediction, dictating thoughts to be recorded

Spark some interest in this story with this prereading activity. Draw a large hand outline on a sheet of chart paper. Cut out a red heart from construction paper and label it "The Kissing Hand." Glue the heart to the center of the hand outline. Show students the cover of the book and lead them to understand that the characters shown on the cover are a mother and her child. Ask youngsters to tell you what they think the story will be about. Write each student's response around the hand. Then share the sweet story with students. After reading, revisit the chart to see which predictions were correct. Then let each child share what special things his parents, grandparents, or caregivers would do to help him feel better in the same situation. Write students' responses on the hand. Post the chart and refer to it when a youngster is feeling a little blue. A reminder of a loved one just might be the pick-me-up a little one needs!

It's raccoons. Patti
It's about love. Sasha
It's about going to school the first time. Alex
She gets me toys.
She kisses me.
My mom makes cookies.
The Kissing Hand
She gives cards.
It's about animals. Rex
She hugs me.
The mama loves the baby. Jeff
It's about nighttime. Cally

Wastebasket Worries

Using language to discuss feelings

Preschoolers can experience a whole sea of feelings when starting school. Help ease their worries with discussions and then toss those worries in the trash! After reading the story, have students brainstorm a list of reasons why they were and Chester is anxious about starting school. Write each child's worry on a piece of paper and then have students line up. Position a wastebasket a few feet from the group. Have each child crumple his paper and then toss it toward the wastebasket until he makes it in. Encourage little ones to cheer as each worry makes it into the trash!

I don't know anyone.

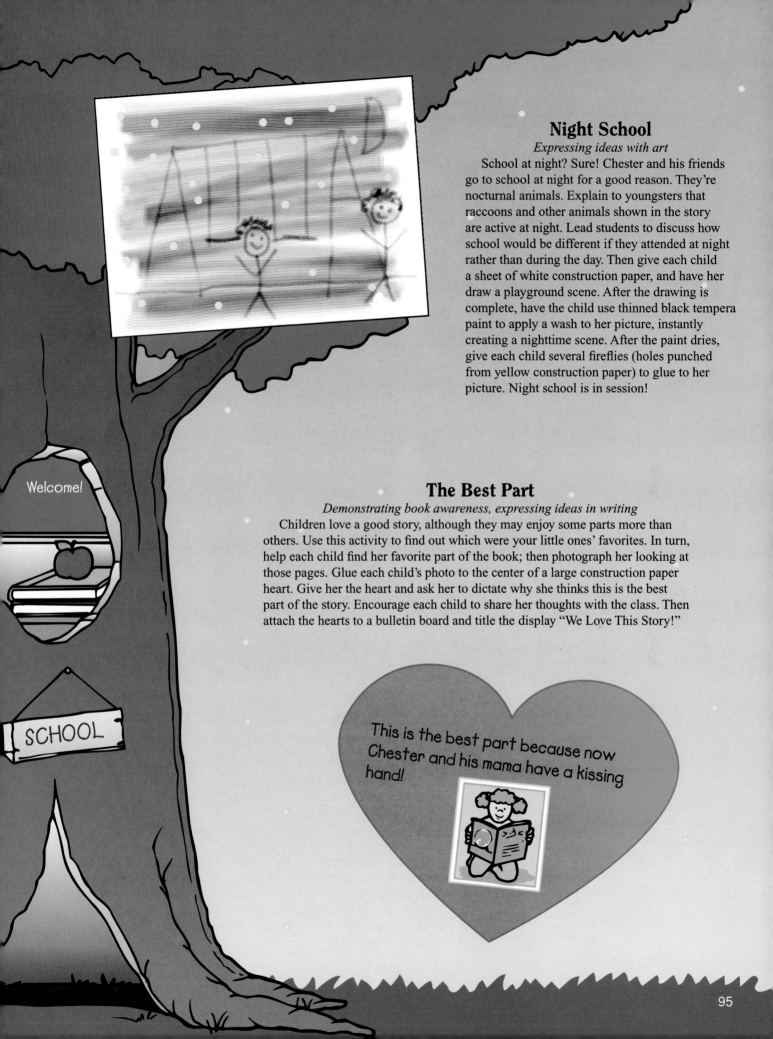

Night School
Expressing ideas with art

School at night? Sure! Chester and his friends go to school at night for a good reason. They're nocturnal animals. Explain to youngsters that raccoons and other animals shown in the story are active at night. Lead students to discuss how school would be different if they attended at night rather than during the day. Then give each child a sheet of white construction paper, and have her draw a playground scene. After the drawing is complete, have the child use thinned black tempera paint to apply a wash to her picture, instantly creating a nighttime scene. After the paint dries, give each child several fireflies (holes punched from yellow construction paper) to glue to her picture. Night school is in session!

The Best Part
Demonstrating book awareness, expressing ideas in writing

Children love a good story, although they may enjoy some parts more than others. Use this activity to find out which were your little ones' favorites. In turn, help each child find her favorite part of the book; then photograph her looking at those pages. Glue each child's photo to the center of a large construction paper heart. Give her the heart and ask her to dictate why she thinks this is the best part of the story. Encourage each child to share her thoughts with the class. Then attach the hearts to a bulletin board and title the display "We Love This Story!"

This is the best part because now Chester and his mama have a kissing hand!

Go Away, BIG GREEN Monster!

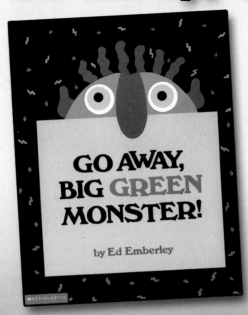

Written & Illustrated by Ed Emberley

Yikes! Yellow eyes, purple hair, and sharp white teeth sure sound scary! But not to worry! This big green monster doesn't hang around too long. In fact, thanks to the clever cutout pages of the book, the big green guy leaves just as quickly as he appears! Follow up this engaging tale with these monstrously fun learning opportunities.

by Roxanne LaBell Dearman
Western NC Early Intervention Program for Children Who Are Deaf or Hard of Hearing, Charlotte, NC

Now You See Him; Now You Don't!
Demonstrating understanding, identifying colors

After one or two oral readings of the story, give your youngsters another way to make the big green monster appear and go away! In advance, make a tagboard cutout of each pattern on page 98. Then, using the book as your reference, trace each cutout onto the appropriate color of felt. Cut out the felt shapes for use on your flannelboard. Display the green face first. Next, have students take turns adding one felt cutout at a time, naming the feature and its color as the piece is positioned. When the monster face is assembled, have everyone shout, "Go away, big green monster!" Then have more student volunteers describe and remove felt pieces one by one until the monster is gone!

I have green hair and a red nose!

Which Monster Am I?
Following directions, identifying colors

Colorful monsters take shape during this activity! To prepare, copy page 98 onto six different colors of construction paper. Laminate the copies for durability and then cut out the patterns. Ready the six face patterns for flannelboard use and display them. Next, have students build each monster face by adding features (with Sticky-Tac adhesive) in the specific colors you request. For example, ask a child to place a blue nose on the orange face or add purple eyes to the yellow face. When the six monsters are assembled, describe individual monsters using color clues such as "I have yellow hair and a blue mouth. Which monster am I?" You'll have plenty of preschoolers eager to point out monsters! Leave the colorful beasts intact for use with "Missing Monster" on page 97.

Bowling for Monsters
Gross-motor development, color matching, counting

Here's a learning game with fun to spare! Remove the lids and labels from six empty 20-ounce plastic soda bottles. Partially fill each bottle with play sand and secure its lid in place. Next, copy the monster patterns from page 98 onto six different colors of construction paper and make six construction paper circles to match. Laminate the patterns for durability and cut them out. Tape each assembled face pattern to a soda bottle. Then use clear Con-Tact covering to adhere the circles to the floor in the shape of a triangle.

To play, a child sets the soda bottle pins in place, matching each monster face to the circle of the same color. Then he stands a distance away and says, "Go away, monsters!" while he rolls a small ball toward the pins. Encourage each bowler to count how many monsters "went away" (were knocked down) and how many are left. Very fun!

Missing Monster
Visual memory, color identification

Use the monsters assembled in "Which Monster Am I?" on page 96 to test your little ones' visual memories. (Or make six different-colored copies of the monster patterns on page 98, cut out each pattern, and assemble the faces.) Begin by displaying three monsters for students to observe. Next, shield the monsters from the class and have the students say, "Go away, monster!" as you secretly remove one monster. Then show preschoolers the two remaining monsters and ask them to name the face color of the missing beast. When youngsters show repeated success, add more monster faces to further challenge their memories!

Build-a-Monster Snack
Fine-motor development, color identification

After a full day of chasing monsters, your preschoolers are sure to have monstrous appetites! Satisfy them with this monster treat! Give each child a green construction paper cutout of the monster face pattern from page 98 and a small cup of Fruit Loops cereal. Have each child place cereal pieces onto the face cutout to form the monster's eyes, nose, and mouth. When she's finished, she tells each edible monster feature to go away ("Go away purple eyes!") and then eats that feature. If she has remaining cereal, she builds another face and enjoys another tasty snack. Yum!

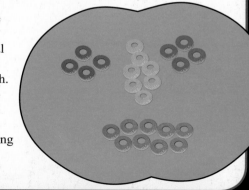

Monster Face and Facial Features Patterns

Use with "Now You See Him; Now You Don't!" and "Which Monster Am I?" on page 96 and "Bowling for Monsters," "Missing Monster," and "Build-a-Monster Snack" on page 97.

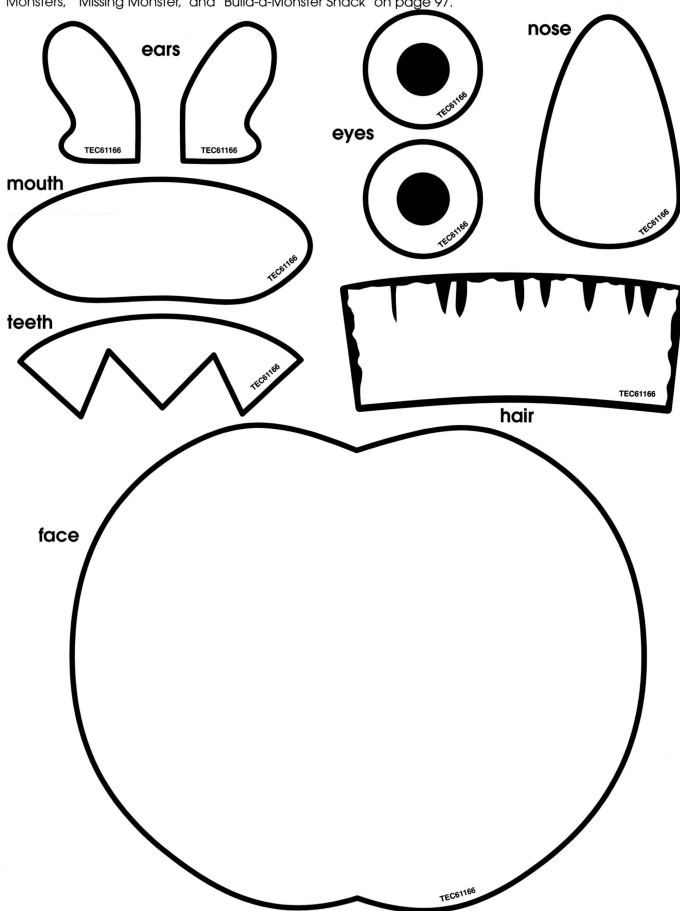

ears

TEC61166

TEC61166

eyes

TEC61166

TEC61166

nose

TEC61166

mouth

TEC61166

teeth

TEC61166

hair

TEC61166

face

TEC61166

The Best of The Mailbox® Preschool • ©The Mailbox® Books • TEC61166

The Runaway Bunny

Written by Margaret Wise Brown
Illustrated by Clement Hurd

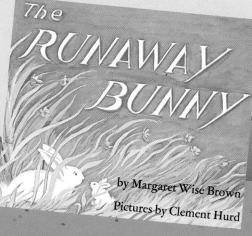

When a little bunny suggests imaginative ways he might run away from his mother, she replies with equally inventive ways to find him! Expand this warm tale of a mother's love with activities that keep youngsters running back for more!

ideas contributed by Roxanne LaBell Dearman—Preschool Western NC Early Intervention Program for Children Who Are Deaf or Hard of Hearing Charlotte, NC

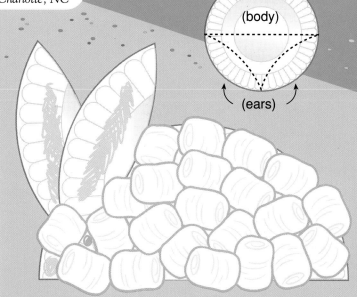

(body)

(ears)

New Disguises

Extending the story, developing fine-motor skills
Little bunny's imagination runs wild thinking of ways to hide from his mother! Your little ones can have loads of fun dreaming up bunny disguises too! For some furry inspiration, help each child make a bunny craft like the one shown. To do this, cut two ears and a body from a thin white nine-inch paper plate. (See the diagram.) Have the student color the inside of each bunny ear and color an eye and a nose on the body. Next, staple the ears to the body and invite the child to glue cotton balls on his bunny's body for fur. Then suggest that the child hold his bunny prop as he describes for you how this bunny might hide from its mother. Write his description on a sentence strip. Then display the sentence strip along with his bunny on a bulletin board titled "More Disguises for *The Runaway Bunny!*"

My bunny will be a big white balloon!

Act It Out!

Dramatizing a story through pantomime
From sailing to tightrope walking, the bunnies from the story are always on the move! Bring your little ones into the action during an animated second reading. To begin, show students each of the book's color illustrations and invite them to suggest ways they could act out the actions of one or both bunnies (for example, flapping their arms when little bunny pretends to fly like a bird). Then read the book a second time, pausing at each color illustration for children to add their actions. Look at the busy bunnies!

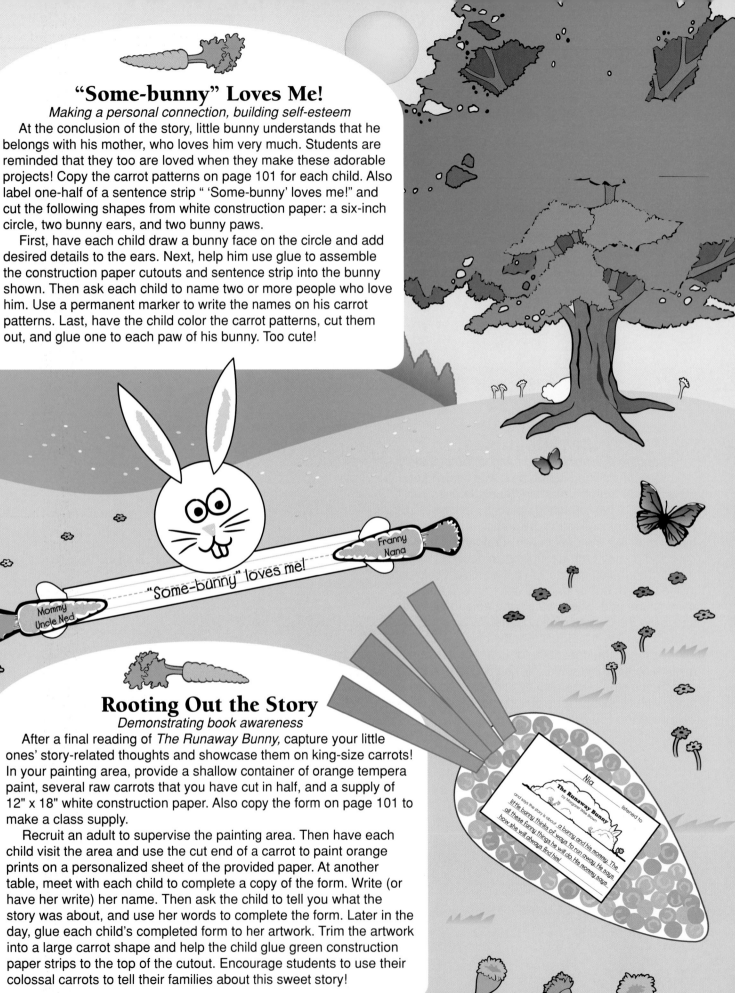

"Some-bunny" Loves Me!
Making a personal connection, building self-esteem

At the conclusion of the story, little bunny understands that he belongs with his mother, who loves him very much. Students are reminded that they too are loved when they make these adorable projects! Copy the carrot patterns on page 101 for each child. Also label one-half of a sentence strip " 'Some-bunny' loves me!" and cut the following shapes from white construction paper: a six-inch circle, two bunny ears, and two bunny paws.

First, have each child draw a bunny face on the circle and add desired details to the ears. Next, help him use glue to assemble the construction paper cutouts and sentence strip into the bunny shown. Then ask each child to name two or more people who love him. Use a permanent marker to write the names on his carrot patterns. Last, have the child color the carrot patterns, cut them out, and glue one to each paw of his bunny. Too cute!

"Some-bunny" loves me!

Franny
Nana

Mommy
Uncle Ned

Rooting Out the Story
Demonstrating book awareness

After a final reading of *The Runaway Bunny,* capture your little ones' story-related thoughts and showcase them on king-size carrots! In your painting area, provide a shallow container of orange tempera paint, several raw carrots that you have cut in half, and a supply of 12" x 18" white construction paper. Also copy the form on page 101 to make a class supply.

Recruit an adult to supervise the painting area. Then have each child visit the area and use the cut end of a carrot to paint orange prints on a personalized sheet of the provided paper. At another table, meet with each child to complete a copy of the form. Write (or have her write) her name. Then ask the child to tell you what the story was about, and use her words to complete the form. Later in the day, glue each child's completed form to her artwork. Trim the artwork into a large carrot shape and help the child glue green construction paper strips to the top of the cutout. Encourage students to use their colossal carrots to tell their families about this sweet story!

Carrot Patterns and Story Form

Use the carrots with " 'Some-bunny' Loves Me!" and the story form with "Rooting Out the Story" on page 100.

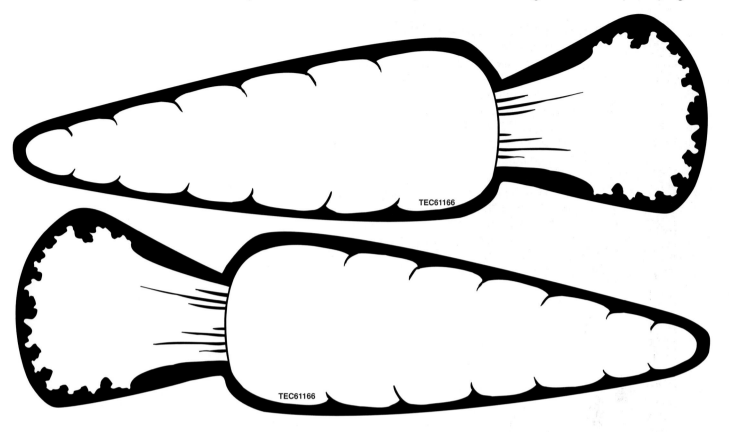

TEC61166

TEC61166

The Best of The Mailbox® Preschool • ©The Mailbox® Books • TEC61166

- -

_____ listened to

The Runaway Bunny
by Margaret Wise Brown

and says the story is about _____

_____

_____

_____

Fish Eyes:
A Book You Can Count On

Written and illustrated by Lois Ehlert

A little black fish explores a sea of colorful friends in this counting extravaganza! The clever cutout eyes of the fish he meets and the subtle addition skills incorporated in the story make this book appealing to all. So dive right in; the water is fine!

ideas contributed by Suzanne Moore, Tucson, AZ

Movin' to the Motion
Building prior knowledge
Fish in the story flip, dart, and jump and so can your youngsters with this engaging prereading activity! To begin, explain that fish move in many different ways. Tell students that some fish dart, moving suddenly and quickly. Then encourage children to move about the room like darting fish. Have little ones suggest other ways fish might move, encouraging them to demonstrate each movement. Then lead students in performing the song shown before they settle in for a read-aloud of the story.

(sung to the tune of "Head and Shoulders")

I can move just like a fish. (See me jump!)
I can move just like a fish. (See me dive!)
Jumping up and diving down,
I can move just like a fish. (Swish! Swish!)

Fish With Flair
Dictating information to complete a sentence
The book's narrator wishes she could be a fish and then imagines what other fish she might see. With this idea, your little ones use their imaginations in a similar way. To prepare, enlarge a copy of a fish pattern on page 104; then make a class supply. Program for each child a sentence strip with the prompt shown. Encourage each youngster to cut out his fish and then decorate it with craft items. Next, ask him to describe his finished fish. As he does, write his response on a strip to complete the prompt. Finally, display the fish and corresponding strips on a wall with the title "If I Were a Fish."

I'd see <u>fish with sparkly stripes</u>.

One Fish, Two Fish
Counting to 10

These fish frolic in a beautiful blue sea just as the fish in the book do! Cover a tabletop with blue plastic wrap to resemble water. Glue green strips of crepe paper down the middle of the water to represent seaweed. Use the patterns on page 104 to make ten colorful fish cutouts. Then place the cutouts to one side of the seaweed. To play, a child visits the table and counts aloud as he "jumps" each fish to the other side of the seaweed.

Match and Munch
Matching items one-to-one

The colorful eye cutouts in this book are sure to intrigue your little ones. After youngsters have had an opportunity to investigate the cutouts, invite them to this sweet math center! Make ten construction paper fish cutouts using the patterns on page 104. Then hole-punch an eye for each fish. Place the fish at a center along with a cup of colorful loop cereal. When a child visits the center, have her put one cereal piece on each fish eye. Then give her a fresh cup of cereal to snack on!

Plus Me!
Dramatizing the story

The little black fish adds himself to the number of fish on various pages. With this idea, youngsters add you to a group! Have a child stand and pretend to be a fish. Lead youngsters in reciting the first four lines of the chant below as the volunteer moves her arms as if they were fins. During the final line of the chant, stand next to the child and move your arms in a similar way. Then help the children count both you and the volunteer to make a total of two fish. Have the youngster sit down. Then repeat the process, inviting two new students to pretend to be fish and changing the number in the rhyme appropriately.

Teacher: How many fish are swimming in the sea?
Children: [One] little fish is/are swimming in the sea.
Teacher: [One] fish?
Children: Yes, [one!]
Teacher: [One] fish plus me!

Fish Patterns
Use with "Fish With Flair" on page 102 and "One Fish, Two Fish" and "Match and Munch" on page 103.

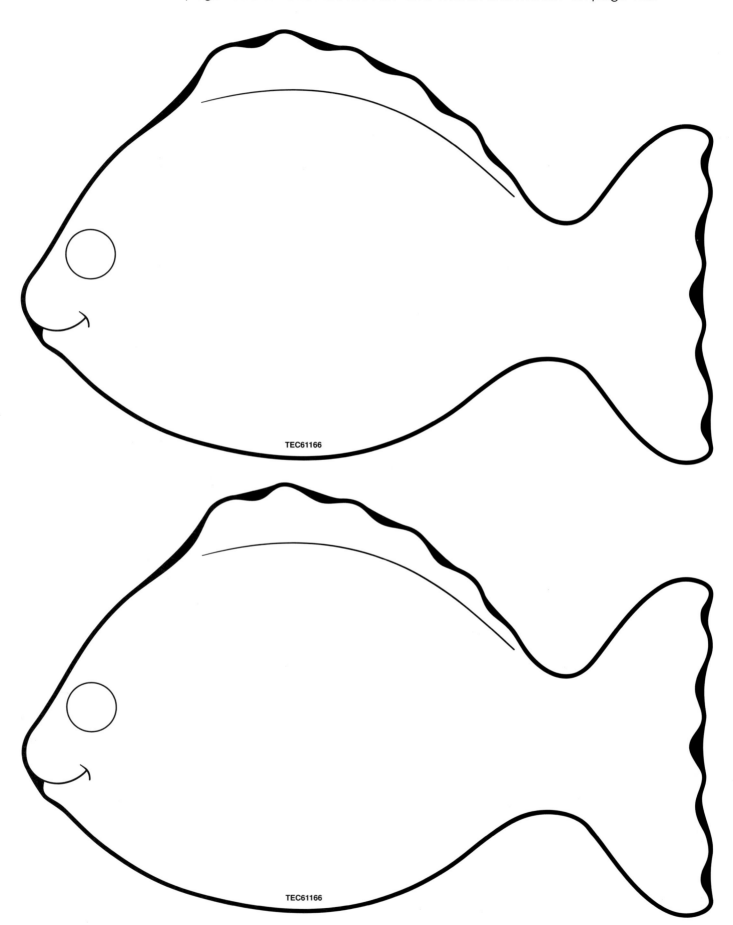

TEC61166

TEC61166

The Best of The Mailbox® Preschool • ©The Mailbox® Books • TEC61166

CENTER UNITS

"A-peel-ing" Birthday Centers

When youngsters visit these birthday-themed centers,
they're sure to have more fun than a barrel of monkeys!

ideas contributed by Ada Goren, Winston-Salem, NC

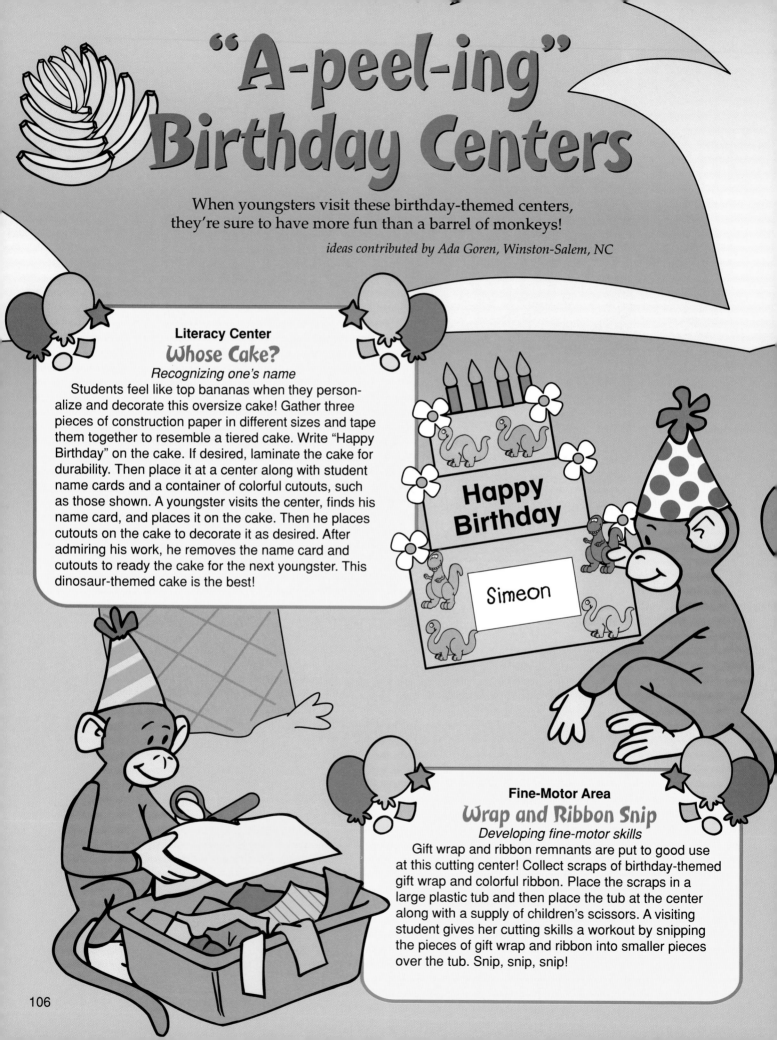

Literacy Center
Whose Cake?
Recognizing one's name

Students feel like top bananas when they personalize and decorate this oversize cake! Gather three
pieces of construction paper in different sizes and tape
them together to resemble a tiered cake. Write "Happy
Birthday" on the cake. If desired, laminate the cake for
durability. Then place it at a center along with student
name cards and a container of colorful cutouts, such
as those shown. A youngster visits the center, finds his
name card, and places it on the cake. Then he places
cutouts on the cake to decorate it as desired. After
admiring his work, he removes the name card and
cutouts to ready the cake for the next youngster. This
dinosaur-themed cake is the best!

Happy Birthday

Simeon

Fine-Motor Area
Wrap and Ribbon Snip
Developing fine-motor skills

Gift wrap and ribbon remnants are put to good use
at this cutting center! Collect scraps of birthday-themed
gift wrap and colorful ribbon. Place the scraps in a
large plastic tub and then place the tub at the center
along with a supply of children's scissors. A visiting
student gives her cutting skills a workout by snipping
the pieces of gift wrap and ribbon into smaller pieces
over the tub. Snip, snip, snip!

Puzzle Center
Plenty of Plates
Developing spatial skills

Serve up spatial skills with sturdy puzzles made from decorative birthday plates! Obtain several decorative plates with different themes. (You may wish to send a note home with youngsters asking parents to send in decorative plates left over from previous birthday celebrations.) After you've gathered several different plates, puzzle-cut each one into two or three pieces. Place the pieces for each puzzle in separate resealable plastic bags and place the bags at a center. A child chooses a bag, removes the pieces, and then reassembles the plate. When he's finished, he puts the pieces back in the bag and chooses a new puzzle.

Art Center
Balloon Prints
Expressing oneself through art

Flour-filled balloons make wildly unique print-making materials! Place the open end of a balloon around the bottom of a funnel. Partially fill the balloon with flour. Then remove the funnel and tie a knot in the end of the balloon. Fill other balloons with flour in a similar way. Place each balloon at your art center next to a shallow tray of tempera paint. Have an adult helper stationed at the art center. A youngster visits the center, presses a balloon into the paint, and then makes several prints on a sheet of colorful paper. He repeats the process with other balloons and colors of paint. When his project is dry, he draws strings on the balloons and glues pieces of colorful confetti to the paper. What fun!

Sensational Snowmen

When it's cold outside, nothing's hotter for your centers than snowmen! Youngsters will warm up to these fun centers in no time!

ideas by Suzanne Moore, Alvin, TX

Literacy Center

Snowman Match

These sassy snowmen will perk up your flannelboard center and reinforce letter-matching skills too. To prepare, make six copies of the snowman and hat patterns on page 111. Color each snowman's buttons and hat and label each pair with a matching letter as shown. Laminate the patterns and then cut them out. Attach a piece of self-adhesive felt to the back of each pattern to ready it for flannelboard use. Place the patterns in a basket near a flannelboard. Invite a pair of children to the center. In turn, have each child draw a snowman and hat from the basket. Instruct him to look at the letter on each pattern and determine whether they match. If they do, have him attach the patterns to the flannelboard. If they don't match, instruct him to return the patterns to the basket. Have his partner check his work and then switch roles.

Dramatic Play

Build It

There's no snow required for this clever snowman-building activity! In advance, stuff several small, medium, and large white plastic bags with newspaper or packing peanuts. Use permanent markers to draw faces on the small bags and to draw buttons on the medium-size bags. Then invite youngsters to don their mittens and get busy pretending to roll and stack the snowballs to build snowmen. Building snowmen couldn't be more fun!

108

Colorful Snowmen

Who said snowmen have to be white? In advance, stock your art center with a supply of large round coffee filters and three bowls of water tinted with food coloring (red, blue, and yellow). Give each child three coffee filters and have her stack and then fold them several times. Instruct her to dip each corner of the filters into a different bowl of colored water. Help her unfold the filters and lay them on paper towels or newsprint to dry. Encourage students to name the colors they see on the filters. They'll be surprised to discover colors other than red, yellow, and blue. Explain to little ones that when two colors mix, a new color is made.

After the filters have dried, cut one of each child's filters into a smaller circle. Have each student glue her filters into a snowman shape on a 12" x 18" sheet of construction paper. Stock the center with plenty of craft materials to complete these colorful snow characters, such as crayons, pom-poms, sticky dots, crepe paper, construction paper scraps, and glue. Mount the completed projects on a bulletin board titled "Colorful Snowmen."

Copycat Snowmen

No two snowmen are alike—except the ones you'll find created by students at this center. In advance, cut two large snowman shapes from poster board. Stock your blocks center with the snowman shapes. To play, pair students and have one child use blocks to make a face on his snowman cutout. Then have him add blocks to represent buttons. Next, encourage his partner to duplicate the snowman, using the same number and colors of blocks. Have the two students clear their snowman shapes and start again, this time with the other child designing the snowman to be copied. Snowman twins—cool!

Snowy Dough

Brrr! It's cold outside! Bring some of the coldness into your classroom with this chilly play dough idea. Begin by mixing up a batch of your favorite play dough; then knead in some iridescent glitter. Chill the play dough in the refrigerator before placing it in your play dough center. Encourage your little ones to roll the dough into balls to make snowmen. Stock the center with rolling pins, plastic snowman cookie cutters, craft sticks (snowman arms), and craft foam facial feature cutouts.

Sand Table

Snowmen—Beach Style

No snow? No worries! Simply dampen the sand in your sand table and provide various sizes of ice-cream scoops along with craft sticks and twigs, and encourage students to create snowmen—beach style! Have each child gently use the point of a pencil to "draw" facial features on her snowman. For added interest, provide miniature straw hats, found at your local craft store, and lengths of ribbon to serve as snappy scarves for these sandy snowmen.

Just Add Eyes

Your little ones will really enjoy throwing themselves—and a couple of black pom-poms—into this easy-to-create center. Begin by drawing a large snowman on bulletin board paper and then taping it to the floor in a corner of your classroom. Add facial features to the snowman, using orange vinyl tape for the nose and black tape for the mouth and buttons, but do not add eyes. Stock the center with two black jumbo-size pom-poms (eyes). Have each child stand on a designated spot and toss each pom-pom eye onto the snowman. If he misses, have him try one more time before passing the eyes to the next child. Fun!

TEC61166

TEC61166

A Rainbow

Brighten up your classroom with this colorful collection of center ideas that are sure to please!

ideas contributed by Ada Goren, Winston-Salem, NC

Math Center

Color Search
Matching colors
Each youngster contributes to this vivid tabletop rainbow! Tape colorful strips of bulletin board paper to a tabletop to resemble a rainbow. Place scissors, glue, and a supply of magazine pages (or grocery store circulars) at the table. A youngster looks through the pages to find pictures that match the colors of the strips. When she finds a picture, she cuts it out, identifies the color, and then glues it in place. Beautiful!

Literacy Center

Rainbow Rubbings
Identifying letters
Write the word *rainbow* in black marker on several tagboard strips. Then trace the letters with thick lines of white glue. When the glue is dry, tape the strips to a tabletop. Stock the center with unwrapped crayons, tape, and a supply of white copy paper. A visiting child feels the letters and names any he recognizes. Then he tapes a sheet of paper on top of the strip (provide help with taping as needed). Finally, he rubs a variety of colorful crayons over the paper.

# of Centers

Writing Center

Color Favorites
Connecting spoken language with written words
Make a class supply of the poem pattern on page 115. Place the poems at a center along with 12" x 18" sheets of construction paper, crayons, and glue. Arrange for an adult to assist youngsters at this center. When a child visits the center, the adult reads the poem aloud and writes the youngster's dictated responses on the lines. Then the student glues her poem to the bottom half of a sheet of construction paper and draws corresponding pictures above the poem as shown.

My Rainbow Rhyme

My favorite color of the rainbow is green

It's the color of frogs , you see,

And the color of leaves . Yippee!

More than the rest,

I like green the best!

Snack Center

Cup of Colors
Following directions
This fruity snack serves up a rainbow of colors! Place at a center separate bowls of strawberry slices, mandarin orange sections, pineapple pieces, green grape halves, blueberries, and purple-tinted whipped topping. A child places a tablespoon of each fruit in a clear plastic cup and then tops it with a scoop of whipped topping. What a tasty rainbow!

Sensory Center

Scoop and Search
Using the sense of touch to explore objects
Fluffy clouds are hidden in this rainbow of rice! To prepare, mix a small amount of rubbing alcohol and food coloring in a large resealable plastic bag. Then add rice and shake the bag until it is thoroughly coated. Pour the rice on paper towels to dry. Prepare several additional colorful batches of rice in the same manner. Pour the prepared rice in a large plastic tub and mix in several cotton ball clouds. Place near the tub several sieves with large holes. A child chooses a sieve and then uses it to scoop up some of the mixture. As the rice funnels through the sieve, it leaves behind the fluffy clouds!

adapted from an idea by Teresa Gmerek
Glendale Head Start
Flinton, PA

Art Center

Colorful Collage Headband
Using a variety of media

Youngsters showcase their favorite colors with this vibrant headband. Place at a center a supply of colorful construction paper strips labeled with color words as shown. Also provide access to glue and a variety of craft materials, such as tissue paper, sticky dots, gift ribbon, and craft feathers. A child chooses a strip and then glues materials of the same color to the strip. When the glue is dry, size the strip to fit the child's head. These creative headbands are tops!

Fine-Motor Area

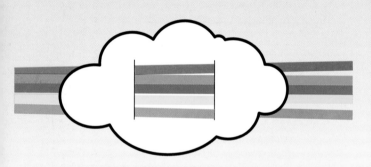

Cloud Weaving
Developing fine-motor skills

This simple weaving project is a visual delight! For each child, make two parallel cuts in a large cloud cutout as shown. Place the clouds and a large supply of colorful construction paper strips at a center. A child weaves as many strips through the cloud as desired. Then he glues the strips in place (provide assistance with gluing as needed).

Gross-Motor Area

Toss the Rainbow
Developing gross-motor skills

To make a rainbow tossing toy, poke a hole through the lid of a film canister. Thread colorful lengths of curling ribbon through the hole. Then knot the ribbons together under the lid and snap it on the canister. Attach two large cloud cutouts to your floor, making sure they are several feet apart. Place the canister on a cloud. A pair of students visits the center, and each child stands behind a different cloud. One child tosses the rainbow toward his partner's cloud. The other youngster retrieves the rainbow and tosses it back toward the other cloud. Students continue tossing the rainbow as time allows.

My Rainbow Rhyme

My favorite color of the rainbow is _____.

It's the color of _____, you see,

And the color of _____. Yippee!

More than the rest,

I like _____ the best!

The Best of The Mailbox® Preschool • ©The Mailbox® Books • TEC61166

Note to the teacher: Use with "Color Favorites" on page 113.

Send In the

Floppy shoes? Red noses? Big silly hats? The clowns must be in town! Engage little ones in this collection of clown-themed centers, and you're sure to see miles of smiles!

ideas contributed by Roxanne LaBell Dearman
Western NC Early Intervention Program for Children Who Are Deaf or Hard of Hearing
Charlotte, NC

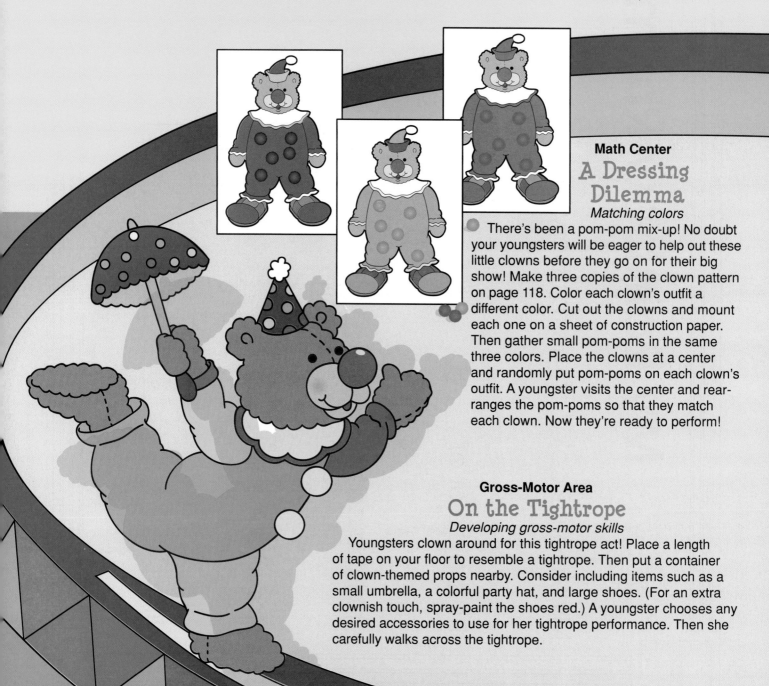

Math Center

A Dressing Dilemma
Matching colors

There's been a pom-pom mix-up! No doubt your youngsters will be eager to help out these little clowns before they go on for their big show! Make three copies of the clown pattern on page 118. Color each clown's outfit a different color. Cut out the clowns and mount each one on a sheet of construction paper. Then gather small pom-poms in the same three colors. Place the clowns at a center and randomly put pom-poms on each clown's outfit. A youngster visits the center and rearranges the pom-poms so that they match each clown. Now they're ready to perform!

Gross-Motor Area

On the Tightrope
Developing gross-motor skills

Youngsters clown around for this tightrope act! Place a length of tape on your floor to resemble a tightrope. Then put a container of clown-themed props nearby. Consider including items such as a small umbrella, a colorful party hat, and large shoes. (For an extra clownish touch, spray-paint the shoes red.) A youngster chooses any desired accessories to use for her tightrope performance. Then she carefully walks across the tightrope.

Clown Centers!

Fine-Motor Area

A Good Hair Day!
Developing fine-motor skills

Clowns need to have bright, colorful hair—and this clown is no exception! Draw a large clown face and collar, similar to the one shown, on a piece of bulletin board paper. Tape the paper to a table. Then place on the table a container of construction paper scraps along with scissors and glue. Each youngster cuts several pieces of construction paper and then glues them to the clown's head. Wow! Look at all that hair!

Snack Center

Crunchy Clown Hats
Following directions

This splendid treat is supersimple! A child visits the snack table and places loop cereal on a colorful clown hat cutout similar to the one shown. When a desired effect is achieved, he nibbles on his tasty decorations!

Block Center

Fantastic Formations
Developing spatial skills

When you attach clowns to your building blocks, youngsters can arrange them to show spectacular clown gymnastics! Reduce the clown on page 118 to make a card the size of your building blocks. Make several copies. Cut out each card and laminate it for durability. Then tape each card to a separate block and place the blocks at a center. Students visit the center to build formations with these cute clowns!

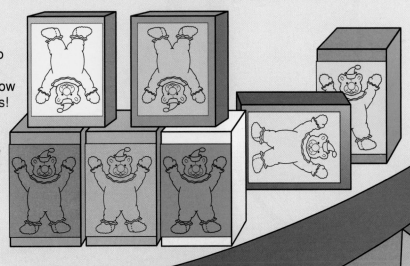

117

Clown Pattern

Use with "A Dressing Dilemma" on page 116 and "Fantastic Formations" on page 117.

TEC61166

The Best of The Mailbox® Preschool • ©The Mailbox® Books • TEC61166

DEVELOPMENTAL UNITS

Preschool Pals

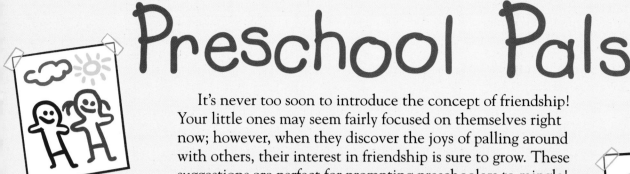

It's never too soon to introduce the concept of friendship! Your little ones may seem fairly focused on themselves right now; however, when they discover the joys of palling around with others, their interest in friendship is sure to grow. These suggestions are perfect for prompting preschoolers to mingle!

Be a Friend

Use this upbeat song to get students in tune with friendship! There'll be loads of smiling and clapping, which is sure to increase self-esteem. For added fun, pair each preschooler with a pal and sing the song another time or two. When it's time to clap, have the pals clap their hands together! Isn't friendship fun?

Friend to Friend

(sung to the tune of "If You're Happy and You Know It")
If you want to be a friend,
Clap your hands! *(clap, clap)*
If you want to be a friend,
Clap your hands. *(clap, clap)*
When you smile every day,
And you're kind in every way,
Then you ARE a special friend.
Clap your hands! *(clap, clap)*

Me Too!

Spur-of-the-moment group sorts are a fun way to promote friendships! On a moment's notice, gather students in your circle-time area. Announce two opposing descriptions such as "I have a cat" and "I do not have a cat." Then help students sort themselves into two groups that represent the descriptions. It's a great way for students to discover classmates with whom they share likenesses. And there's an excellent chance that some follow-up conversations will take place. My cat's name is Patches. What is your cat's name?

Building a Friendship

Building a friendship takes time. It also takes cooperation! This center activity provides a foundation for both! Use masking tape to designate a building area in your block center. Each day ask a different small group of students to cooperatively build a block structure inside the designated area. As the youngsters work, make their praiseworthy behaviors known to the class. Then photograph each group of builders with its completed structure. When all students have been photographed, tape the photos to a sheet of poster board titled "Friendship Builders." Display the resulting poster as a positive reminder of important friendship qualities.

A Friendly Chat

Increase your little ones' understanding of friendship by asking an adult friend to visit your classroom. Introduce your friend and explain how and when the two of you met. In a relaxed conversation, share stories about your friendship. Describe how the two of you are alike and different, and explain ways in which you help each other. Also talk about the importance of laughing, listening, and forgiving in a friendship. If possible, show students snapshots of the two of you together. Students will be delighted to know that their teacher has such a special friend, and no doubt their understanding of friendship will grow too.

Fingerpainting Pals

Favorite colors and friends go hand in hand during this fingerpainting project! Have preschoolers visit the art center in pairs. Provide one large sheet of fingerpaint paper and a variety of fingerpaint colors for each twosome. Ask the pair to create a colorful painting together, making sure that the artwork incorporates the favorite colors of both painters. When the painting is dry, cut it in half, and write each child's name and the date on each half. Then send each partner home with a reminder of his special painting project. Students are sure to agree that painting with a pal is loads of fun!

Happy Face, Sad Face, Silly Face, Mad Face

Poke around this pumpkin patch and you'll quickly discover that it's ripe with emotions! Use these ideas revolving around jack-o'-lanterns for a seasonal look at the many feelings your young preschoolers experience.

by Sue Fleischmann—Child and Family Specialist,
Waukesha County Project Head Start, Waukesha, WI

A Feelings Forecast

Identifying feelings, graphing

Can three little pumpkins help youngsters get a feel for their feelings? You bet! Use a black permanent marker to decorate the pumpkins with three different faces: a happy face, a sad face, and a neutral face sporting a straight line for a mouth. Next, cover a tabletop with paper, draw a three-column grid on the paper, and place the three pumpkins on the grid as shown. Give each child a die-cut paper pumpkin to place on the grid in front of the real pumpkin whose face matches her mood. When everyone has contributed to the graph, discuss the results. Later, remove the pumpkin cutouts so the activity can be repeated again!

...very proud

Faces and Feelings

Expressing feelings

Smiles, frowns, and pouts make appearances during this feelings investigation! Teach students this simple song, encouraging each child to make a face that portrays the featured feeling. After the verse, invite little ones to share times when they feel this way. Plan to repeat the verse a few times, each time substituting a different feeling, such as *mad, proud, scared, sad,* and *silly.* Look at me!

(sung to the tune of "Mary Had a Little Lamb")

I am feeling very [glad],
Very [glad], very [glad].
I am feeling very [glad].
See it on my face!

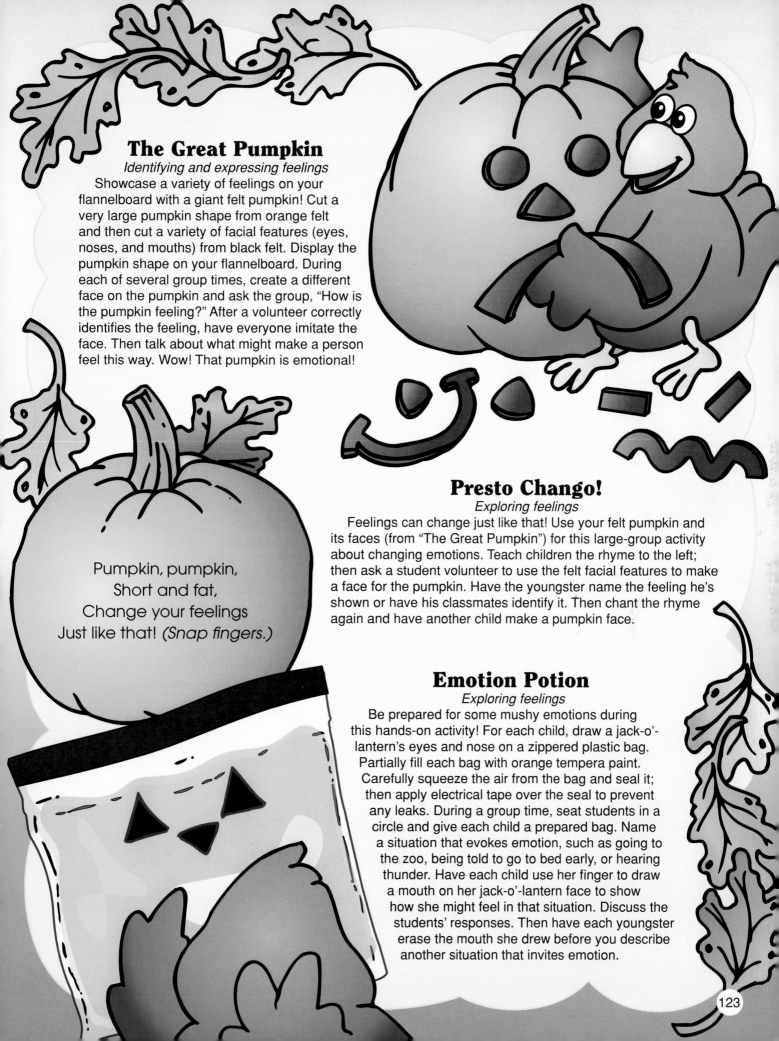

The Great Pumpkin
Identifying and expressing feelings
Showcase a variety of feelings on your flannelboard with a giant felt pumpkin! Cut a very large pumpkin shape from orange felt and then cut a variety of facial features (eyes, noses, and mouths) from black felt. Display the pumpkin shape on your flannelboard. During each of several group times, create a different face on the pumpkin and ask the group, "How is the pumpkin feeling?" After a volunteer correctly identifies the feeling, have everyone imitate the face. Then talk about what might make a person feel this way. Wow! That pumpkin is emotional!

Pumpkin, pumpkin,
Short and fat,
Change your feelings
Just like that! *(Snap fingers.)*

Presto Chango!
Exploring feelings
Feelings can change just like that! Use your felt pumpkin and its faces (from "The Great Pumpkin") for this large-group activity about changing emotions. Teach children the rhyme to the left; then ask a student volunteer to use the felt facial features to make a face for the pumpkin. Have the youngster name the feeling he's shown or have his classmates identify it. Then chant the rhyme again and have another child make a pumpkin face.

Emotion Potion
Exploring feelings
Be prepared for some mushy emotions during this hands-on activity! For each child, draw a jack-o'-lantern's eyes and nose on a zippered plastic bag. Partially fill each bag with orange tempera paint. Carefully squeeze the air from the bag and seal it; then apply electrical tape over the seal to prevent any leaks. During a group time, seat students in a circle and give each child a prepared bag. Name a situation that evokes emotion, such as going to the zoo, being told to go to bed early, or hearing thunder. Have each child use her finger to draw a mouth on her jack-o'-lantern face to show how she might feel in that situation. Discuss the students' responses. Then have each youngster erase the mouth she drew before you describe another situation that invites emotion.

Taking Care of ME!

Little ones' self-help skills increase by dinosaur-size proportions as they discover different ways they take care of themselves. Most likely this new knowledge will prompt a "dino-mite" celebration of self-esteem too!

ideas contributed by Sue Fleischmann—Child and Family Specialist
Waukesha County Project Head Start, Waukesha, WI

I Can Exercise!

Jump-start your investigation of self-help skills with an action song. Share with youngsters that not only is exercise fun, but it's good for the body too! Explain that exercise helps people feel better and even think better! Start with the provided verse, and then sing additional verses, spotlighting a different movement during each rendition. (See the suggestions provided.) What a fun way to care for oneself!

Make Time for Exercise!
(sung to the tune of "My Bonnie Lies Over the Ocean")

Oh, exercise helps build our muscles.
It keeps our hearts healthy and strong.
If everyday we work our bodies,
Our bodies can help us live long.

[Stretch. Stretch. Stretch. Stretch.]
Let's work our bodies and sing along.
[Stretch. Stretch. Stretch. Stretch.]
Let's work to be healthy and strong!

Other movements include *march, hop, lunge, twist,* and *skip.*

I Can Wash My Hands!

The importance of hand washing becomes clear during this sparkling demonstration! To show how germs can spread, rub glitter gel (or glitter lotion) on your hands. Then, as youngsters make their way to circle time, invite them to shake one of your hands. When students are seated, find out who has glitter on their hands. Tell students that when you shook their hands, the glitter spread from your hands to theirs. Explain that germs spread in a similar way, and this is why it is so important to wash one's hands at specific times during the day, such as before eating. Set aside time for each child to wash his hands using soap and water. Afterward, do a quick hand check to make sure all the glitter is gone. Then have students settle in for an oral reading of *Wash Your Hands* by Tony Ross. Little ones will surely be informed—and amused!

I Can Choose Healthy Snacks!

Remind little ones that choosing healthy snacks is a great way to take care of themselves! To prepare, collect a variety of food pictures and wrappers, making sure your collection contains both healthy and unhealthy snack choices. Mount the pictures and wrappers on construction paper cards and then laminate the cards for durability. Also program two paper grocery bags, one with a smiling face and one with a frowning face. Roll down the top of each bag, as desired.

During circle time, ask students to help you sort the food cards by placing healthy snacks in the smiling bag and unhealthy snacks in the frowning bag. As each food card is sorted, invite a volunteer to tell why the food pictured is or is not a good snack choice. For a befitting follow-up, let each youngster make a healthy snack.

A banana is good for me.

Snack Sort

For an independent-learning extension of "I Can Choose Healthy Snacks!" attach a smiley-face sticker to the back of each healthy snack and a frowning-face sticker to the back of each unhealthy snack. Place the self-checking cards and grocery bags at a center for students to sort independently.

I Can Brush My Teeth!

Preschoolers probably know that they are taking care of themselves when they brush their teeth. However, do your little ones understand how clean teeth help them stay healthy? To be sure, copy a tooth pattern like the one shown onto white construction paper to make a class supply. Cut out each pattern. Next, set up a paint station that includes a shallow container of white tempera paint and a clean toothbrush. During group time, ask little ones why they brush their teeth. Lead them to conclude that they brush their teeth for the same reason they wash their hands: to get rid of germs! Then invite each child to take a turn at the paint station. While at the station, he uses the white paint and toothbrush to brush away each pesky germ shown on a tooth cutout.

125

Buzzin' Around the Hive!

Gross-Motor Activities for Busy Bees

When warm, sunny weather has little ones abuzz with energy, make a beeline for these sweet suggestions! Your youngsters will have a honey of a time showing off their gross-motor moves as they buzz about!

by Ada Goren

Garden Moves

Performing specific movements, color recognition

These large and colorful blooms keep little bees on the move! Cut large flower shapes from different colors of construction paper. Add desired details to the flowers; then use clear Con-Tact covering to attach them to the floor in open classroom areas. For a small-group activity, meet students at the classroom hive (circle-time area). Give each bee a different instruction, such as "Tiptoe to the blue flower" or "Hop to the red flower." When each bee is on his flower, have the bees buzz back to the hive for another round of play. Or, when one little bee needs to release extra energy, ask him to perform specific gross-motor movements as he buzzes from flower to flower! Buzz, buzz!

Freeze, Bees!

Responding to tempo with creative movement, making quick stops

Keep a recording of Rimsky-Korsakov's "Flight of the Bumblebee" handy, and you have a honey of a movement activity at your fingertips! Simply gather your little honeybees at the hive (circle-time area), start the music, and invite the youngsters to dance and move to the music. Sporadically stop the music and say, "Freeze, bees!" As your little honeys try to freeze their bodies in midmovement, applaud their gross-motor control. Freeze, bees!

"Bee-boppin' "
Creating and performing a sequence of gross-motor movements

How does a bee do the "bee-bop"? Any way a preschooler decides! Remind the class that honeybees get their food from flowers. Explain that when a honeybee discovers yummy flowers, it buzzes back to the hive and does a little dance to tell the other bees where the flowers are. For a fun movement activity, have each of your little bees make up a short dance that includes three different movements, such as *twist, clap, jump, clap, jump*. Invite interested preschoolers to teach their dances to the rest of the hive. *Stomp, stomp, wiggle, wiggle, clap, clap!*

Hunting for Honey
Performing specific movements in cooperation with others

Buzz outdoors for this movement activity, which promises sweet results! In advance, hide a sealed box of Honeycomb cereal in a shady area of your outdoor playground. Then, before taking your youngsters outside, tell them a sweet surprise awaits them. All they must do is carefully follow your instructions. Next, give the group a series of movements to perform, beginning with tiptoeing outdoors. End the activity by guiding the group to where the cereal is hidden. Who's ready for a sweet snack?

"Bee-utiful" Balance
Developing balance

Here's a honey of an idea for developing balance! On a paved outdoor surface, use wide chalk to draw a giant bee shape such as the one shown. Invite children to walk heel to toe along each stripe on the bee. Encourage enthusiastic bees to walk in the same manner along the curved lines of the wings. When a little one successfully walks the lines of the bee, award her a badge that reads "[child's name] has 'bee-utiful' balance!"

Buzzy has "bee-utiful" balance!

Honeybee Hopscotch
Performing one- and two-foot hops, developing balance

Without a doubt, this bee-themed hopscotch game will be the buzz of the playground! Use chalk to draw a hopscotch grid on a paved area. Draw a beehive at the starting point and a colorful flower in each box. Also provide a yellow beanbag for pollen. A visiting bee tosses the beanbag on the grid. He starts at the hive and hops to the end of the grid, where he turns around. Then he hops back, pausing to collect the pollen before returning to the hive. Encourage your little bees to alternate turns with their bee buddies.

"Bee-ware" of the Bear!
Demonstrating gross-motor movement, playing cooperatively

During this large-group game, busy bees protect their hives from a large honey-loving bear! In an open area, spread out several plastic hoops—approximately one hoop for every two or three students. Ask students to pretend that each hoop is a hive filled with honey. Explain that their job is to guard the honey from a big honey-loving bear! To guard the honey, one or more bees must be inside each hive. To begin play, direct youngsters to buzz around the open area demonstrating a designated gross-motor movement. After several seconds of play, say, "Oh, no! Here comes the bear!" Wait until each hive is safely guarded before announcing that the bear was scared away. Then direct the youngsters to once again buzz around outside the hives and perform a specific gross-motor movement. Uh-oh! The bear is back!

Precious Pollen
Performing specific movements

When your little bees have energy to spare, send them pollen collecting! For an indoor game, use the flower blooms made for "Garden Moves" (page 126). For an outdoor game, use colorful chalk to draw large colorful blooms on a paved surface. Place a nonbreakable bowl on each flower and then place in each bowl a supply of paper punches to represent pollen. Have a child start at a designated hive location and then follow your directions to move from flower to flower. For example, you might ask her to hop to the first flower, march to a second one, and gallop to a third. After she reaches each flower, she gathers a few pieces of pollen in a small plastic zippered bag. When she returns to the hive, she exchanges her bag of pollen for a tasty honey-flavored snack such as Honey Nut Cheerios cereal!

Literacy Units
ABCD

That's My Name!

To a preschooler, the most meaningful word in the world is his name. As he learns the letters of his own name, he begins to notice letters and their sounds in other names and words. Opportunities to recognize names are great literacy builders. This unit contains numerous nifty opportunities to help your preschoolers recognize and learn from their names.

Who's Here?

While they're bright eyed and bushy tailed, have your youngsters find their names as a way of taking the morning's attendance. For each child, program one side of an index card with her name and glue her photo on the other side. Laminate the cards for durability. Each morning, arrange the cards randomly in a pocket chart with students' names facing out. As each child arrives, ask her to find her name card and turn it over to show her smiling face. You can tell at a glance who's at school, and the children will get daily practice finding their names. There's no better way to start the day!

Kristin Niles—PreK ESE
Blackburn Elementary School
Palmetto, FL

My Name Marks the Spot

Call your little ones to circle time anytime with this musical invitation! In advance, prepare a name strip for each child. Invite each youngster to decorate his strip with stickers or stamps. Before circle time, arrange the name strips in your large group area. Then sing the first verse of the song below. Have each child find his name and have a seat! When circle time is over, sing the second verse and collect the name strips as students file past you and return to their seats.

(sung to the tune of "London Bridge")

Find your name and sit right down,
Sit right down, sit right down.
Find your name and sit right down.
Let's have circle time!

Bring your name back up to me,
Up to me, up to me.
Bring your name back up to me.
See you next time!

Wanda R. Hostas—Three- and Four-Year-Olds
God's World Christian Child Care and Preschool
Prescott Valley, AZ

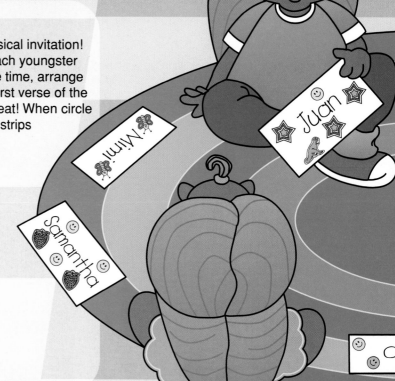

Scurrying Off to Centers

Send students scurrying off to centers with this useful name-recognition transition! Write each child's name on an individual index card. Before center time, scatter the cards randomly on the floor in your group area. Pick up one card at a time and ask if anyone recognizes the name on it as her own. After a child reads her name, invite her to choose a center or proceed to the one already selected. If a child doesn't recognize her name, invite classmates to help read the card or simply say her name; then allow her to choose a center.

Karyn Abele—PreK
Elmwood School
Syracuse, NY

Monica

Monica

Bobby

Shaneeka

Special Name, Special Helper

When a preschooler discovers that he has been selected to be a special helper, he'll have one more reason to consider his name special! First, create a name card for each child in your class. Stack the cards and bind them together with one or two metal rings. When you need a helper, randomly flip to a child's name card, show it to the group, and say, "This child may pick a book for me to read" or "This child may choose the next song we sing." Whenever you reach for the helper cards, your whole class will be eager to read the name you pick! In fact, it will help them learn to identify classmates' names too!

Jennifer Schear—Preschool
Clover Patch Preschool
Cedar Falls, IA

Roberto

Gavin

Where Is My Name?

Here's a name-recognition game you won't want to pass up! Have your little ones sit in a circle; then make each child his own name-and-picture card (or use the ones from "Who's Here?" on page 130). Play some music or simply sing a favorite song as students pass the name cards around the circle. When the music stops, have youngsters hold the cards with the names facing out. Choose a child and have him try to find his own name card. When he selects his name, have the child holding the card flip it over to reveal the picture. If it is the player's name card, he trades the card he's holding for his own card and returns to his spot. If not, he may guess again until he finds his own name.

Destiny Simms—Two- and Three-Year-Olds
Kiddie Academy Learning Centers
Laurel, MD

Magical Rubbings

Your students will really get a feel for their names with this activity, which engages their sense of touch! To prepare, write each child's name on a piece of tagboard. Trace over the letters with thick craft glue or gel glue; then allow the glue to dry thoroughly. Invite each youngster to locate his name strip among the others, run his fingers over the letters to feel their shapes, and name any letters he recognizes. Then have him make a name rubbing. Tape the name strip to a tabletop; then tape a sheet of paper over the strip. Have the child rub the side of a peeled crayon over the entire sheet of paper. Don't miss the look of delight when he sees his name emerge on the paper! It's magic!

Later, encourage children to choose class-mates' names for rubbings too. Some children may start by making rubbings of names that have the same beginning letter as theirs.

Donna Pollhammer—Three-Year-Olds
YMCA Chipmunk Preschool
Westminster, MD

Mobile, Marvelous, and Mine!

These easy-to-make placemats will help your preschoolers with both name recognition and name writing. They're especially useful if you can't permanently label the tables in your room with students' names. To make a placemat, use a colorful sheet of paper with a fun seasonal border around the edge or add interest with stamps or die-cuts. Write a child's name near the center top. Then glue the placemats to tagboard, if desired, before laminating them for durability.

Each day, randomly put the placemats on your tables. Challenge each child to find his name and have a seat. Then pass out dry-erase markers and encourage each youngster to trace over his name and copy his name on the open space on his mat. The marker will wipe right off, and the placemat will be ready for more name recognition and writing practice on another day!

Jennifer Schear—Preschool
Clover Patch Preschool
Cedar Falls, IA

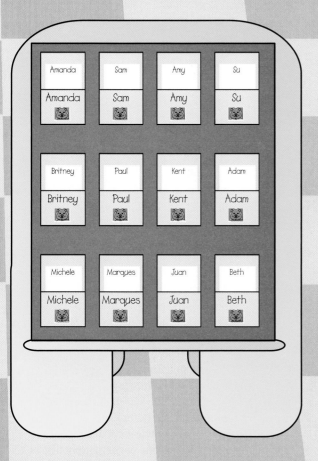

Pick Your Pocket

Make a name pocket for each child, and watch as your little ones not only recognize their names but learn to write their names on their projects too! To prepare, gather a class supply of library pockets. On the front of each one, write a child's first name. Then add a photo of the child. Next, write the child's first name at the top of a 3" x 5" index card (as shown) and slip the card into the pocket. Display all the pockets together in a convenient location in your classroom. When a child needs to write her name on a paper, have her find her name pocket and remove her name card. Instruct her to take her card to her seat, copy her name onto her work, and then return the card to its pocket. After a child has mastered writing her first name, program the card in her pocket to include her last name too!

Brenda Horn—PreK
Livingston Elementary
Livingston, IL

133

A Fine Time for Rhyme

There's no time like the present to help your youngsters wiggle and giggle their way into an understanding of rhyme.

ideas contributed by Mary Lou Rodriguez

Do These Words Rhyme?

Have a few minutes to spare? Slip in this rhyme identification activity! Display a clock or timepiece. Then put your ear near it as if to listen for ticking, and say the verse below, inserting the word pair "red, bed." Determine whether your students hear a rhyming pair. Continue by saying the chant several times, substituting different pairs of rhyming or nonrhyming words and inviting the whole class to respond. Vary the verse by substituting "boys" or "girls" for "children." When youngsters' confidence in their rhyming skills has grown, say the verse a few more times, calling on specific children to answer the question.

Listen, children, because it's time.
Tell me now—do these words rhyme?
[pair of words]

Rhyming Celebration

A little dance of celebration gives an exuberant touch to simple rhyme identification. For this activity, prepare a set of rhyming picture cards for flannelboard use. You will need one card per child. Also set up a tape player near your flannelboard and choose a lively dance song to accompany this activity. Seat students in a semicircle facing the flannelboard and give each child a card. Call out two words that are pictured on the children's cards and ask the youngsters holding those cards to display them on the flannelboard. Have the group say the words and decide whether they rhyme. If the group decides the words do not rhyme, have the pair take the cards and return to their places. If the group thinks the words do rhyme, turn on the music for a moment and invite the standing children to do a little celebratory dance before sitting down. When all rhymes have been identified, displayed, and celebrated, have everyone participate in one last victory dance!

A Pooch With a Taste for Rhyme!

When you put an adorable dog puppet in charge, your little ones will joyfully join in on this rhyming activity. Locate a dog puppet with a moveable mouth or make one by gluing construction paper pieces onto a paper lunch bag. Also gather an assortment of food props and store them in a basket. Begin by having the class say the nursery rhyme "Higglety, Pigglety, Pop" (below) several times with your canine friend. Call children's attention to the rhyming words *pop* and *mop*. Then say the nursery rhyme again, replacing *pop* with a nonsense word that rhymes with one of the food items in the basket. Pause long enough for the puppet to help the children find the food that rhymes with the substituted word. Then have everyone chime in to finish the verse. Repeat this process until each food item has been used in the rhyme.

Higglety, Pigglety, Pop
Higglety, pigglety, *pop!*
The dog has eaten the *mop.*
The pig's in a hurry;
The cat's in a flurry.
Higglety, pigglety, *pop!*

Higglety, pigglety, [nonsense word that rhymes with food]!
The dog has eaten the [food that rhymes with word above].
The pig's in a hurry;
The cat's in a flurry.
Higglety, pigglety, [nonsense word used above]!

Spectacular Spectacles

Grab some goofy goggles or oversized sunglasses. They're all you need to get your little ones excited about this I Spy rhyming game. Begin by having children identify one body part at a time. As the part is identified, have children suggest words that rhyme with that body part. For example, they might suggest "deer" for "ear" or "bed" for "head." Next, don your funky eyewear with a dramatic flourish and announce it's time to play I Spy. Circling around the children, say, "I spy a body part that rhymes with *three.*" Help children conclude that you must be referring to a knee. Continue playing in this manner until several body part rhymes have been identified.

Departure-Time Rhyme

Make the most of every minute by slipping a personalized rhyming song into departure time. During your routine, sing the provided ditty to each youngster. However, instead of singing the child's real name, sing a rhyming substitution. For example, you might sing "Flad" for "Thad" or "Grayla" for "Kayla." After each silly rendition, invite the class to join you in singing an accurate version of the tune for the named child.

Goodbye
(sung to the tune of "Goodnight, Ladies")
Goodbye, [child's name].
Goodbye, [child's name].
Goodbye, [child's name].
We're glad you came today!

Lisa Zartman—Early Childhood Special Education
Blue Ridge Elementary School, Columbia, MO

Special Delivery!
Print Concepts

Deliver an assortment of print concepts with this first-class collection of activities!

ideas contributed by Roxanne LaBell Dearman—Preschool
Western NC Early Intervention Program for Children Who Are Deaf or Hard of Hearing
Charlotte, NC

What's in the Mailbox?

Teach little ones that different kinds of mail are delivered to mailboxes every day! Decorate a box to resemble a mailbox. Next, gather a variety of child-appropriate forms of mail and readdress the mail to your class. Also prepare a letter similar to the one shown that includes your name and the signature of a colleague your youngsters know. Tuck the letter inside an envelope addressed to your class and place the envelope in the mailbox you made. When students arrive, gather them near the mailbox. Sing the provided song, opening the mailbox and identifying the letter as indicated. Read the letter to the class. Then have students share what they know about letters and mail carriers. Each day repeat the process with a different piece of prepared mail. Adapt the song to reflect each item. Youngsters will look forward to this daily discussion of mail!

Dear Mrs. Dearman's Class,

I heard that you are going to be learning about mail carriers. A mail carrier's job is to deliver the mail each day. I know you will enjoy learning about mail carriers and the kinds of mail they deliver.

Sincerely,

Mrs. Murphy

(sung to the tune of "Good Night, Ladies")

What's in our mailbox?	There is a [letter]!
What's in our mailbox?	There is a [letter]!
What's in our mailbox?	There is a [letter]
Let's open it and see!	Addressed to you and me!

Pretty Boy Bird

15 Treetop Way

Bird Nest, NC

Address Success!

Understanding that print has meaning

Student addresses are the focus of this booklet project. After all, mail carriers need addresses in order to deliver mail! To make a booklet for each child, stack two 9" x 12" sheets of white construction paper, hold them vertically, and slide the top sheet upward about one inch. Then fold the papers forward, creating four graduated layers. Staple near the fold. Title the booklet "My Address" and label the bottoms of the booklet pages with the child's name and address.

Invite one or more students to join you at a table. Give each child his prepared booklet. Read the booklet title. Next, help each child read his name. Then have him illustrate his self-likeness on the page. In a similar manner, have the child illustrate his home on the page that shows his street address and on the page that shows his city and state have him illustrate a favorite place there. Youngsters will be bursting with pride when they carry these impressive address booklets home!!

Daily Deliveries
Tracking print from left to right

Through rain, snow, and blowing wind this mail carrier puppet helps youngsters practice tracking print! Copy the provided poem onto chart paper and draw a simple mailbox at the end of each line as shown. Also prepare a mail carrier stick puppet like the one pictured. Introduce the poem and puppet during circle time. Explain that the poem is read in the same direction in which the mail carrier delivers his mail. Then move the puppet from left to right as you read each line of the poem.

Plan to read the poem each day so that the mail carrier puppet can deliver the mail. In time, invite volunteers to move the puppet as you read aloud the poem. Also make the poem and puppet available during playtime so little ones can mimic the mail delivery and practice tracking print!

The Mail

The mail comes in the rain.

The mail comes in the snow.

The mail comes when it's hot,

And even when winds blow.

The mail comes every day

Both up and down the street.

Then mail carriers go back home

To rest their tired feet.

Pretty Boy
1 Treetop Way
Bird Nest, NC

Tweety Bird
2 Treetop Way
Bird Nest, NC

Mail Truck

Mailbag

Mail Carrier Play
Developing an awareness of print

This dramatic-play area will receive your little ones' stamp of approval! Place a shallow box labeled "Mail Truck" on a table. Inside the box place packages, letters, magazines, and other types of child-appropriate mail—each labeled with one of two simple addresses. Position a chair at the head of the table to resemble the seat of a mail truck. Next to the chair set a tote bag labeled "Mailbag." Then provide two mailboxlike containers labeled with addresses that match the mail on the mail truck. Youngsters visit the center to examine the mail, deliver it, and act out the actions of their neighborhood mail carrier.

Mail Truck Melody!

Understanding that words are groups of letters

This activity delivers a truckload of word knowledge and name identification practice! Write each line of the provided song on a sentence strip, leaving blank spaces where indicated. Place the sentence strips in order in a pocket chart. Then write each student's name on a blank card. Also program individual cards with the following: a square, a star, "D," and "2."

Gather students near the pocket chart. Explain that the song on display is missing two words. Remind students that most words contain two or more letters. Ask student volunteers to point to words on the chart. Also ask volunteers to point to spaces between words. Next, show the class the card programmed with a square. Ask students whether this card shows a word. Lead them to conclude that the card shows a shape, not a word. In a similar manner, evaluate the three remaining cards that do not show words. Finally, show students a name card. When students identify the name as a word, place the card in the pocket chart. Add a second name in a like manner; then lead students in singing the song. Repeat the song several times, replacing the name cards each time. If desired, put a card in the pocket chart that does not show a word. No doubt your little ones will inform you of your error!

(sung to the tune of "I've Been Working on the Railroad")

I've been driving in my mail truck

Each and every day.

I've been driving in my mail truck,

Handing mail out on the way.

Here's a package for _____,

A letter for _____ too!

I'll be driving in my mail truck

Until the day is through.

Jack

Nicki

I like it when the mail carrier brings me a letter from my nanna.

Letters of Appreciation

Associating spoken words with written words

After learning about mail carriers for a few days, invite your preschoolers to talk about what they've learned. Review with the class the job of a mail carrier and invite youngsters to name different kinds of mail that mail carriers deliver. Follow up the class discussion by meeting with small groups of students. Ask each child to tell you something she would like a mail carrier to know. Write her name and her comment on a sheet of paper and then have her illustrate her written message. When every child has completed a project, gather the students together. As they watch, slide the projects into a large envelope addressed to the local post office or to your neighborhood mail carrier. Your preschoolers will be pleased as punch to have created a parcel for mailing. And you'll feel grand about introducing the children to several concepts of print!

Name _____

Here Comes the Mail!

The Best of The Mailbox® Preschool • ©The Mailbox® Books • TEC61166

Note to the teacher: Use this page as a fun follow-up to "Daily Deliveries" on page 137. Have each child trace the dots from left to right.

Learning Letters and Sounds

Little ones are sure to come out of their shells for these simple ideas that encourage them to make connections between letters and their sounds!

Snail Trails

This small-group activity has an adorable snail guide! Color and cut out a copy of the snail cards on page 143. Choose a letter familiar to your youngsters; then write the letter on each of four sheets of tagboard. Next, trace each letter with white glue. When the glue is dry, gather a group of up to four youngsters and give each child a snail and a letter. Explain that the snail has made a trail that looks like a letter. Help students identify the letter and say its sound. Then have each child move her snail along the trail as she repeats the letter's sound.

Roxanne LaBell Dearman
Western NC Early Intervention Program for
   Children Who are Deaf or Hard of Hearing
Charlotte, NC

The Letter-Pokey

Here's a twist on a familiar tune, which has little ones up and dancing with letters! Give half of your youngsters cards labeled with the letter *R*; then give the remaining half cards labeled with the letter *J*. (Or use different letters as desired.) Lead students with the letter *R* cards in performing the song shown. When the song is finished, help students identify the letter's sound. Then repeat the process with students who have the letter *J* cards, changing the song appropriately. For extra letter-sound reinforcement, have the two groups of students switch cards; then repeat the activity.

(sung to the tune of "The Hokey-Pokey")

You put your [R] in.
You take your [R] out.
You put your [R] in,
And you shake it all about.
You hold up letter [R] as you're dancing all around.
What is this letter's sound?

Deborah Garmon, Groton, CT

Smell a Sound

Reinforce letter sounds with a "scent-sational" small-group activity! Poke small holes in the lids of four film canisters. Gather coffee grounds, pieces of buttered popcorn, and slices of a lemon and ripe banana. Place each food item in a different canister. Then label each canister with the first letter of the item's name and replace the lids. Gather a small group of youngsters and explain that you have a mystery item that begins with the letter *B.* Have students review the sound of the letter *B.* After each child has had an opportunity to smell the corresponding canister, have youngsters suggest what the item might be. Congratulate them when they guess it's a banana. Then repeat the process with each remaining canister.

Roxanne LaBell Dearman

Disappearing Pages

This simple illusion will delight your little ones! Obtain a small photo album. Then insert a different letter card in each pocket in the first half of the album. Leave the second half of the album blank. Flip the album over so the last page is now the first page and present it to your youngsters. Reveal several of the blank pages as you explain that you filled the album with letters and now they're missing. Encourage youngsters to close their eyes and make a wish that the letters would reappear.

While their eyes are closed, flip the album so it's facing the correct direction. When students open their eyes, open the album and express relief that the letters have returned; then help students identify each letter and its sound. Youngsters are sure to ask for repeated reviews of this fantastic idea!

Shelley Hoster
Jack and Jill Early Learning Center
Norcross, GA

Sack-Lunch Sounds

Color and cut out a copy of the food cards on page 144. Ready the cards for flannelboard use and then place them on your flannelboard. Label one lunch-size paper sack with the letter *P* and a second sack with the letter *S*. Place the sacks near the flannelboard. To begin, have youngsters identify the letters and their sounds. Then encourage a child to choose one of the food items from the board and say its name. Prompt the child to decide whether the word begins with /p/ or with /s/. Then have her place the item in the corresponding bag. Continue in the same way with each item on the flannelboard. These lunches are all packed!

Adapted from an idea by Nancy Morgan
Care-A-Lot In-Home Daycare and Preschool
Bremerton, WA

Sound Swat

Place three letter cards on your floor (cards for the letters *F, M,* and *T,* for example); then gather a group of youngsters in front of the cards. Review the names of the letters and their sounds. Then give a youngster an unused flyswatter. Invite the youngster to swat the letter that makes the /f/ sound. Continue in the same way for several rounds, giving each youngster an opportunity to swat different letters.

Karen Eiben
The Learning House Preschool
La Salle, IL

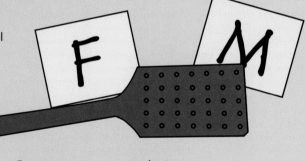

Letter on a Stick

Youngsters take ownership of letters and sounds with this whole-group activity. Glue each of several letter cards to a different craft stick to make stick puppets. Give each puppet to a different child. Encourage one of the youngsters to hold up his puppet for all to see. Help youngsters identify the letter. Then lead them in singing a version of the song below, inserting the appropriate student name, letter, and sound. Continue in the same way with each youngster in possession of a puppet.

(sung to the tune of "Mary Had a Little Lamb")

Anna's *B* says /b/, /b/, /b/,
/b/, /b/, /b/, /b/, /b/, /b/.
Anna's *B* says /b/, /b/, /b/.
The sound of *B* is /b/.

Christy McNeal
Hudson Elementary, Hudson, IA

Food Cards

Use with "Sack-Lunch Sounds" on page 142.

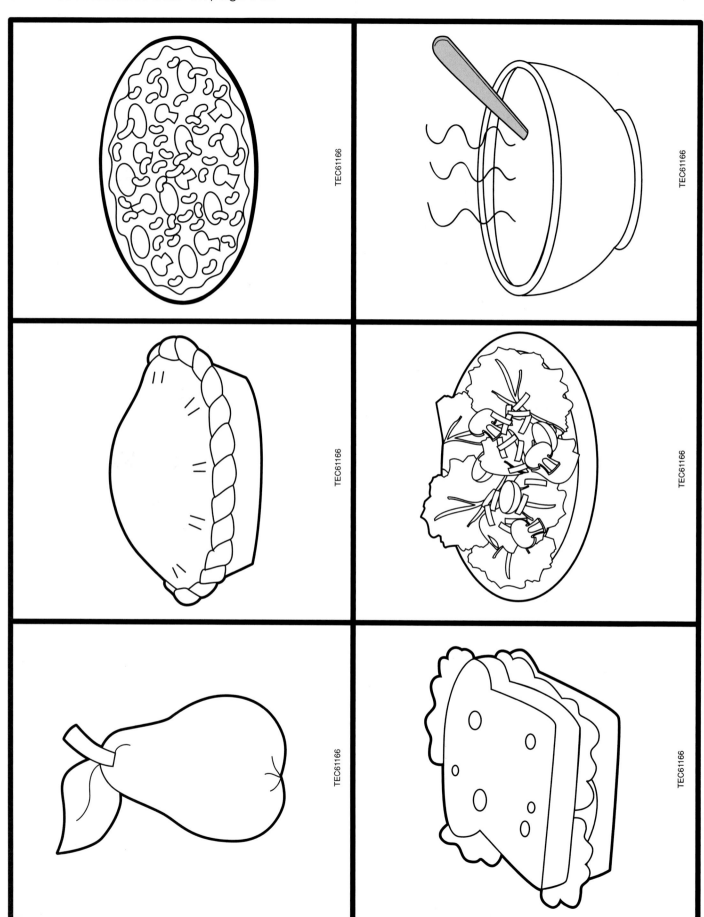

The Best of The Mailbox® Preschool • ©The Mailbox® Books • TEC61166

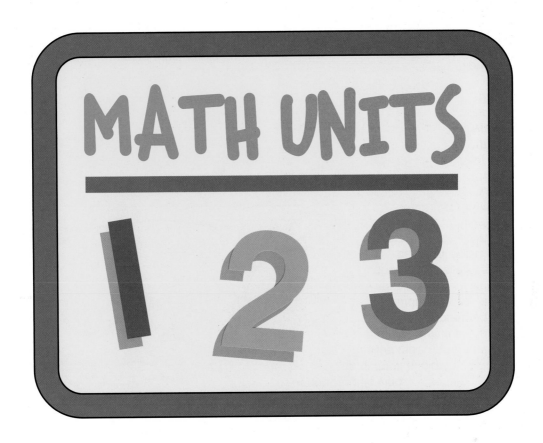

M-M-M-Math With Cookies!

Match them, munch them, count them, crunch them! Cookies are key in this batch of math explorations—baked especially for back-to-school sampling!

by Ada Goren

Comparing shapes

Cookie to Cookie

Try this tasty exploration of three basic shapes! Diagonally slice Fig Newton cookies to create triangle shapes. Arrange a class supply of the shapes on a paper plate. Then fix a plate of rectangular cookies and a plate of round cookies. Show the class the three plates of cookies. Ask your little ones to describe the three cookie shapes by telling how the shapes are alike and how they are different. Identify the shapes as triangles, rectangles, and circles. Next, serve every child one cookie of each shape. Then invite preschoolers to nibble on their circles, triangles, and rectangles. Who knew an investigation of shapes could be so yummy!

Sorting shapes

Cookie Jar Visitors

Who's *putting* cookies in the cookie jar? Your youngsters, that's who! To prepare this shape-sorting center, make three construction paper cookie jar shapes and one white construction paper copy of the cookie patterns on page 149. Label each cookie jar with a different shape as shown. Then color the patterns, laminate them for durability, and cut them out. Store the cutouts at the center. A student sorts the cookies "into" the jars with the corresponding shapes. Now who *takes* the cookies from the cookie jar? Yes, that's you!

Rolling in Dough

Stir up another batch of shape-matching practice at your play dough center! Gather cookie cutters in several basic shapes and an aluminum cookie sheet. Use a permanent marker to trace each cookie cutter shape onto the cookie sheet. Place the cookie sheet, the cookie cutters, a rolling pin, and a spatula at your play dough center. Each visiting baker rolls out some play dough. He cuts the dough with a selected cookie cutter, uses the spatula to lift the cookie shape, and then positions the shape on the cookie sheet atop the corresponding outline. He repeats this process until each outline is covered with a cookie. Cookies, anyone?

One-to-one correspondence

One per Cookie, Please!

At this play dough center, one-to-one correspondence takes center stage! Provide a batch of play dough and a variety of large, colorful, solid manipulatives. Encourage young bakers to form balls of dough and then press a colorful centerpiece into each dough ball. While it may be customary for more seasoned bakers to press candy kisses or gumdrops in their cookies' centers, your little ones are sure to be just as thrilled with their colorful creations. If desired, place a cookie sheet at the center so each baker can line up his freshly formed goodies.

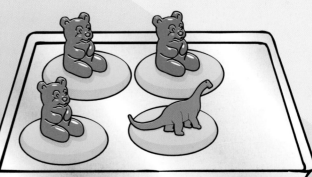

147

Counting to ten

From Zero to Ten

Preschoolers work up an appetite participating in this clever counting poem! At your snack table provide for each child a paper plate and a napkin holding ten minicookies (or pieces of Cookie Crisp cereal). Slowly recite the poem, allowing ample time for little ones to count their cookies onto their plates. At the conclusion of the poem, the cookies go down the hatch! Keep a supply of cookies on hand because your little ones will definitely want to do this again!

Counting Cookies

Zero cookies on my plate? *(points to plate)*
That's not right—just you wait! *(looks at teacher)*
Here's one cookie, two cookies, three cookies, and four, *(counts cookies onto plate)*
Five cookies, six cookies, seven cookies, now more. *(counts cookies onto plate)*
Eight cookies, nine cookies, and one more makes ten! *(counts cookies onto plate)*
Ten cookies! Let's eat and do this again! *(moves tongue over lips)*

Counting objects

Cookie Sheet Counting

One, two, three, four…counting cookies is no chore! In fact, it's fun! To prepare for this small-group counting activity, make a tagboard copy of the cookie patterns on page 149. Color the cookies, cut them out, and then attach a small piece of magnetic tape to the back of each one. You will also need a metal cookie sheet and a set of magnetic numbers.

Gather a small group of youngsters. Hold the cookie sheet on your lap, facing the students. Place two tagboard cookie cutouts on the sheet and invite a student volunteer to count them. Next, place a magnetic "2" on the sheet with the cookies. Talk about why this numeral describes the cookies on the cookie sheet. Repeat the procedure using varying numbers of cookies until each child in the group has had a turn counting. Challenge capable preschoolers to find the matching magnetic numbers themselves. Impressive!

Cookie Patterns
Use with "Cookie Jar Visitors" on page 146 and
"Cookie Sheet Counting" on page 148.

TEC61166	TEC61166	TEC61166	TEC61166
TEC61166	TEC61166	TEC61166	TEC61166
TEC61166	TEC61166	TEC61166	TEC61166
TEC61166	TEC61166	TEC61166	TEC61166
TEC61166	TEC61166	TEC61166	TEC61166
TEC61166	TEC61166	TEC61166	TEC61166

Patterning
in Preschool

Join these prickly little hedgehogs for a heap of pleasing patterning practice!

ideas contributed by Angie Kutzer, Garrett Elementary, Mebane, NC

> **Rustle, swish, rustle, swish!**

Leafy Loudness

What do youngsters hear when they run through a pile of leaves? Rustle, swish, crackle, crinkle! Why not use these fun leafy sounds for some fall-inspired patterning practice! Begin by chanting a simple AB sound pattern, such as rustle, swish, rustle, swish, encouraging youngsters to chime in when they're ready. Continue with other sound patterns, using the words mentioned above. When students are comfortable with this activity, encourage them to pretend to walk through piles of leaves as they recite the patterns.

Teeny, Tiny Patterns

These student-made patterning strips make simply smashing bracelets! Use decorative hole punches to make a supply of two different shapes. Sort the shapes into containers. Then place the containers at a table along with a supply of 1" x 9" construction paper strips and glue. Encourage each child to place six evenly spaced dots of glue on a strip. Have her place a cutout on each dot to make an AB pattern. When the glue is dry, staple the strip to make a bracelet.

Nancy Foss
Wee Care
Galion, OH

Totally Texturized!

Gather a variety of textured items, such as sandpaper, fake fur, corrugated cardboard, and aluminum foil. Cut the items into small squares. Glue some of the squares to sentence strips to make patterns. Then place the remaining squares in a container. Tape the strips to a tabletop and set the container nearby. A child feels each pattern; then he extends each pattern with the remaining squares. Rough, smooth, rough, smooth!

Nosy Hedgehogs

Make three construction paper copies of the hedgehog cards on page 152. Cut out the cards and laminate them for durability. Gather a supply of black and pink pom-poms and place them in separate containers. Then set the container and cards in a center. To begin, introduce youngsters to this unique little animal with a read-aloud such as *The Prickly Hedgehog* by Mark Ezra or *Hedgie's Surprise* by Jan Brett. Explain that hedgehogs' noses come in several different colors. Next, invite each child to visit the center and lay the cards in a row. Then have her place noses on the cards to make a pattern!

Snackin' on Patterns

Cereal isn't just for breakfast anymore—it's for patterning practice too! Give each child a napkin. Then place a small amount of two distinctly different kinds of cereal on each napkin. Also give each child a strip of paper sectioned into squares similar to the one shown. Encourage each child to place a piece of cereal in each square to make a simple pattern. Then have him munch on his treat.

Hedgehog Cards

Use with "Nosy Hedgehogs" on page 151.

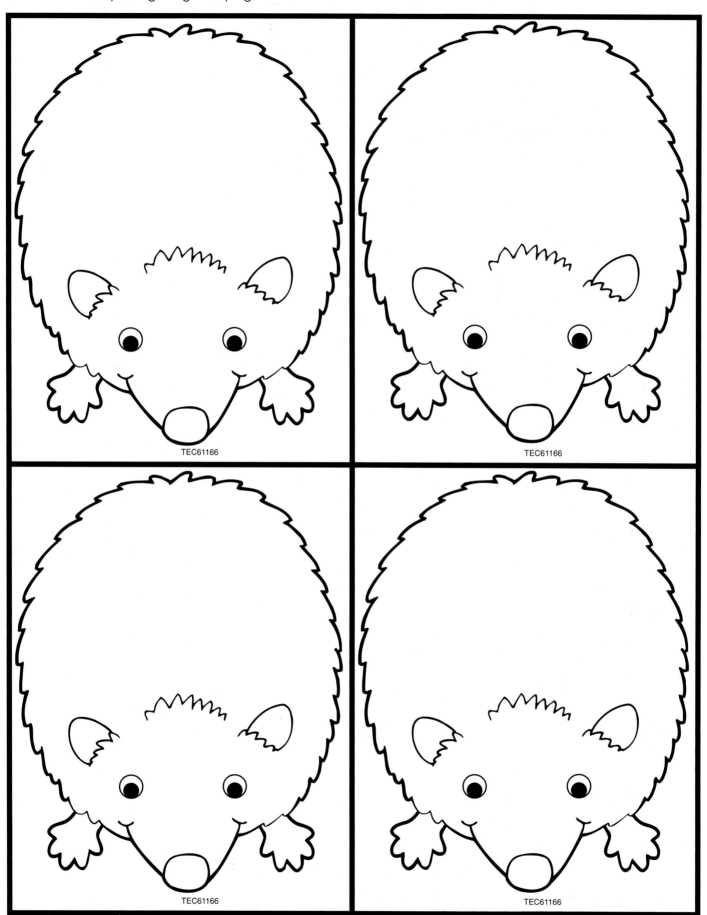

TEC61166

TEC61166

TEC61166

TEC61166

 The Best of The Mailbox® Preschool • ©The Mailbox® Books • TEC61166

One-to-One Correspondence—Something to Bark About!

No bones about it, youngsters will dig this collection of ideas centered around one-to-one correspondence and man's best friends—puppy dogs!

ideas by Roxanne LaBell Dearman, WNC Early Intervention Program for Children Who Are Deaf or Hard of Hearing, Charlotte, NC

Buried Bones

Dig up some one-to-one correspondence practice at your sand table with this easy idea. To prepare, bury a desired number of bone-shaped dog treats in your sand table. Place the same number of plastic dog dishes or bowls nearby. Add a small shovel or scoop to the table for digging. Tell students that puppies have buried bones in the sand table. Invite each child, in turn, to the center and have him dig through the sand to find the bones. As each bone is found, encourage the child to place it in a dog bowl. Have him continue until there is one bone in each dish. Then instruct him to bury the bones in the sand for the next center visitor.

Doggie Dash

Youngsters dash to distribute dog supplies to some furry canine friends with this exercise. Have five children stand in a line. Position five stuffed dogs at the opposite end of your room. Give each child a basket with five identical dog-related items in it, such as clean or new balls, chew toys, leashes, collars, or dog dishes. In turn, have each child walk to the dogs and place one item from her basket in front of each dog. When her basket is empty, have her go to the end of the line and sit down. Continue the dash until each child has distributed her dog supplies. Then discuss with youngsters the items each dog has—one ball, one chew toy, one leash, one collar, and one dish. Lead them to realize that each dog has the same items and the same number of each item. This doggie dash is done!

Bowwow Collars

Every pup needs a collar, and this activity has youngsters taking care of that! To prepare, make two tagboard copies of the tags on page 155. Cut six tagboard strips to serve as collars. Position six stuffed dogs in front of students. Have students help you think of six dog names. Write each name on a different tag. Staple the ends of each strip to make a collar. Next, place the hook side of a Velcro fastener on the back of each dog tag; then put its corresponding loop side on a dog collar. Invite a child to choose a dog's tag and attach it to a collar. Have her put the collar around the neck of a dog of her choice. For older preschoolers, vary the number of dogs and collars. Ask students to complete the activity and then use terms such as *more, less,* and *same* to describe the outcome.

Cozy Canines

Transform your dramatic-play area into a cozy slumber area for pooches. Stock the center with a desired number of stuffed dogs and enough of the following items so that each puppy can have one of each: a cardboard box (dog bed), a small blanket, and a chew toy. Encourage your little pet owners to place one dog into each bed, cover each one with a blanket, and then give each pooch a chew toy. When the pooches wake up, have their masters gather the blankets, toys, and dogs into a large basket for the next visitors at the center. Night-night, doggies!

Play Dough, Pups, and Pals

Transform your play dough center to ready each puppy for a walk—complete with a leash and a collar! To prepare, make several copies of the child and dog patterns on page 155. Color, cut out, and laminate the patterns for durability. Have each child fashion a dog collar from play dough for each dog and then roll another piece of play dough into a rope to make a leash for each one. Instruct him to connect each leash from a dog's collar to a child's hand. Have him continue until each pup is paired with a pal and ready for a walk!

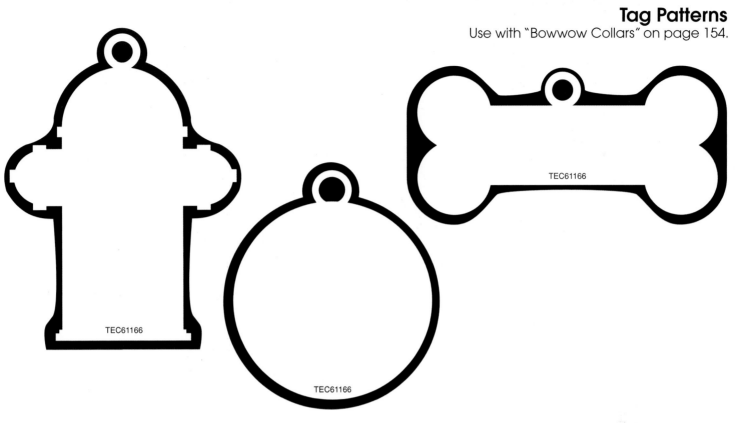

Child and Dog Patterns
Use with "Play Dough, Pups, and Pals" on page 154.

Recognizing Numbers!

Youngsters are sure to flock to these unique number recognition ideas all about that colorful rainforest bird: the toucan!

ideas contributed by Suzanne Moore, Tucson, AZ

Branching Out

How many toucans will perch on this branch? Your little ones find out with this whole-group number game! Englarge one of the toucans on page 158 and cut out ten colorful copies of it. Cut a long branch shape from brown bulletin board paper. Then place the branch and the toucans on the floor in your circle-time area along with a stack of number cards with numerals from 1 to 10. To begin, lead youngsters in reciting the rhyme shown. Then have a child choose a card. After youngsters help him identify the numeral, encourage him to count out the corresponding number of toucans and then place them on the branch. Remove the toucans from the branch and repeat with the remaining number cards.

5

How many toucans will we see
Perched on the branch of the kapok tree?

Three

How Many Eggs?

To prepare for this small-group activity, cut a large hole in an oatmeal canister to resemble a hole in a tree trunk. (You may also wish to paint the canister brown.) Place shredded paper in the trunk to make a nest. Then mold white play dough into four balls to resemble eggs. Gather a small group of youngsters around the nest and explain that a female toucan builds a nest in a hollow tree and lays from two to four eggs. Have youngsters close their eyes as you place two, three, or four eggs in the nest. Then prompt students to open their eyes and say the number of eggs in the nest without counting. After confirming the number by counting, write the corresponding numeral on the board. Repeat the process several times.

Mmm, Berries!

What would a toucan like to eat? Berries are a favorite treat! Color and cut out an enlarged copy of one of the toucans on page 158. Then ready the toucan for flannelboard use. Cut from felt ten round circles to resemble berries. Use a permanent marker to label each berry with a different numeral from 1 to 8. To begin, place the toucan on your flannelboard. Then recite the rhyme with your youngsters, placing the corresponding berries on the board in a row. Finally, ask youngsters questions about the berries, such as "Which berry shows the number 3?"

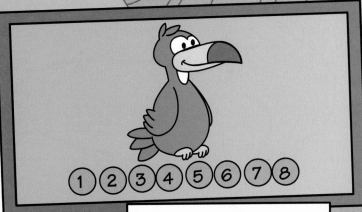

Toucan's hungry. What will he eat?
Berries are a favorite treat.
Feed him one, two, three, and four.
He's still hungry; give him more!
Feed him five, six, seven, eight.
No more berries on his plate!

Fly little flock. Fly high and low.
Fly really fast; then fly really slow.
Fly in a circle; then land on your feet.
Hop, hop, hop, and take a seat.

4

Flocks of Toucans

Gather a set of number cards with numerals from 4 to 10. Hold up a card and have students identify the numeral. Then invite the corresponding number of children to stand and pretend to be a flock of toucans. Lead the flock in performing the chant shown. Then repeat the process with the remaining cards.

Toucan Treats

Make a copy of the math mat on page 158 and label each toucan with a different numeral. Then give each student a copy of the programmed mat and a cup of colorful o-shaped cereal. Have each child identify the first number shown. Then have her count the corresponding number of cereal pieces and place them on the toucan's bill. Encourage her to repeat the process for each number on the page. Finally, invite her to nibble on the tasty toucan treats!

58 **Note to the teacher:** Use with "Branching Out" on page 156 and "Mmm, Berries!" and "Toucan Treats" on page 157.

Get Ready for Graphing

From collecting data to making simple graphs, there are sure to be activities in this unit just perfect for your students' skill level. So pop on those sunglasses and slide into some flip-flops. It's time to get ready for graphing at the beach!

ideas contributed by Lucia Kemp Henry, Fallon, NV

Seashells in the Sand
Collecting data

Before youngsters dive into graphing activities, give them some practice collecting data. Make a class supply of colorful seashell cutouts (see the patterns on page 161). Laminate the cutouts; then scatter them about your classroom. Lead youngsters in singing the song shown. Then have them collect the seashells and place them in a container. When all the seashells have been found, gather youngsters in a circle and dump out the shells. Encourage students to make observations about the shells, noting their various colors and shapes. Finally, place the seashells in your sand table for youngsters to investigate independently.

(sung to the tune of "Take Me Out to the Ballgame")

Take me out to the ocean.
Take me out to the beach.
I see some seashells that look so grand.
I can see them all over the sand.
So let's make a seashell collection.
It's so easy to do.
You just pick up each one you find
Till you have a few!

Who's on the Beach?
Organizing data

To prepare for this large-group activity, use a length of tape to divide your pocket chart into two columns; then label the columns as shown. Cut out two colorful copies of the boy and girl cards on page 162. Place five towels on your floor to represent beach towels. Invite each of five youngsters to choose a towel to lie on and then pretend he's at the beach. (You may wish to provide children's sunglasses to enhance the role-playing.) Lead the remaining students in counting the number of boys and the number of girls at the beach. Then help a child use this information to place the corresponding number of boy and girl cards on the chart. Repeat the process several times with different numbers of boys and girls.

Splendid Starfish
Organizing data

To begin, have each child place a sheet of paper over a piece of sandpaper. Encourage her to rub an unwrapped crayon over the paper to make a sandy beach. Then have her attach five star stickers (starfish) on her beach, making sure to include at least three different colors. Encourage her to name the colors of starfish represented as you write the color words on her paper. Finally, have her count the number of starfish in each color; then help her write the corresponding number after each color word.

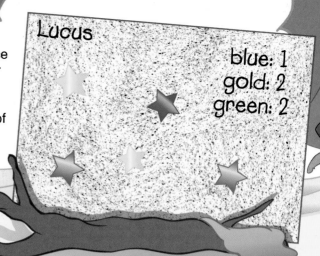

Lucus

blue: 1
gold: 2
green: 2

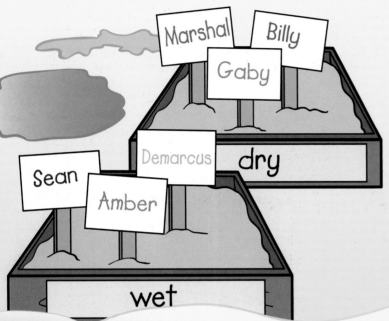

Marshal

Billy

Gaby

Demarcus

dry

Sean

Amber

wet

Dry Sand, Wet Sand
Organizing and interpreting data

Would your youngsters prefer to play with dry sand or wet sand? Place dry sand and moist sand in separate shallow tubs; then label the tubs accordingly. To begin, have each child make a name sign similar to the one shown. Then invite each youngster to touch and manipulate the sand in each tub. When she decides which sand feels more appealing, she places her name sign in the corresponding tub. After all youngsters have had a turn, help them count the number of signs in each tub and compare them using words such as *less, more,* and *same.* Finally, remove the signs and replace them with some beach toys; then place the tubs at a center for independent exploration.

Pretty Pearls
Contributing to an object graph

To prepare for this activity, gather a supply of pom-poms (pearls) in two different colors and place them in a container. Make a simple floor graph from bulletin board paper as shown. Then label the columns to represent the colors of the pearls. With great fanfare, show youngsters your fabulous collection of pearls. Then invite each child to take one from the container. Help each youngster place his pearl on the graph in the appropriate column. Ask students questions about their choices, such as, "Why did you choose to place your pearl in this column instead of the column where Anna placed her pearl?" Finally, help youngsters interpret the finished graph. Then invite each child to take his pearl home.

yellow
pink

TEC61166

TEC61166

TEC61166

TEC61166

TEC61166

TEC61166

TEC61166

TEC61166

THEMATIC UNITS

A Crayon Welcome!

Color your way into a brand-new year of preschool with these crayon-themed ideas!

*ideas contributed by Sue Fleischmann—Child and Family Specialist
Waukesha County Project Head Start, Waukesha, WI*

Tickled Pink!

Before school begins, let your new preschoolers know that you're tickled pink about their arrival! On a copy of page 167, write a brief letter that welcomes the students and tells something about yourself. If desired, request in your note that each child bring to school a small photograph of herself (for use with "A Pack of Preschoolers" or "Crayon Puzzlers" on page 165). Then photocopy the letter on colorful paper to make a class supply. Cut out each copy, fold it as shown, add a personal greeting to the front, and then tuck the letter inside a business-size envelope that you've prepared for mailing. Now that's a special delivery!

Welcome to preschool, Bryanna!

Look Who's Here!
Name recognition

Extend a colorful welcome and promote name recognition with a bit of by-the-door decor! Position a small table near the entry of your classroom and showcase a jumbo crayon cutout close by. Next, write each child's first name on a colorful crayon cutout (pattern on page 168). Laminate the cutouts for durability and adhere the hook side of a Velcro fastener to the back of each one. Place the cutouts on the table, arranging them with the names showing. Within children's reach, post an attendance chart that has two long strips of Velcro loop tape adhered to it.

On the first day, help each child find the crayon with his name, and assist him in attaching it to the attendance chart. During the day, incorporate the crayon cutouts into select circle-time activities. Return the cutouts to the table before students arrive the next school day. Your little ones will soon be identifying their names on their own!

Yahoo for You!

Look Who Is Here!

Deanna · Juan · Njeri

Katie · Ben · Derrick · Amelia · Josh · Carlos

A Pack of Preschoolers!
Oral language, print awareness

Here's a colorful and personalized way to get to know each preschooler in your pack! Make a class supply of page 169. Working with one child at a time, read aloud each unfinished sentence for the student to complete. Write her answers in the spaces provided. Next, have her color the crayon her favorite color. Later, mount each child's snapshot to her completed page. (See "Crayon Crowns" on page 166 for a photo opportunity.)

To make a class book that's certain to be a circle-time favorite, prepare a yellow construction paper cover that resembles a pack of crayons. Bind the pages inside the cover and let the fun begin!

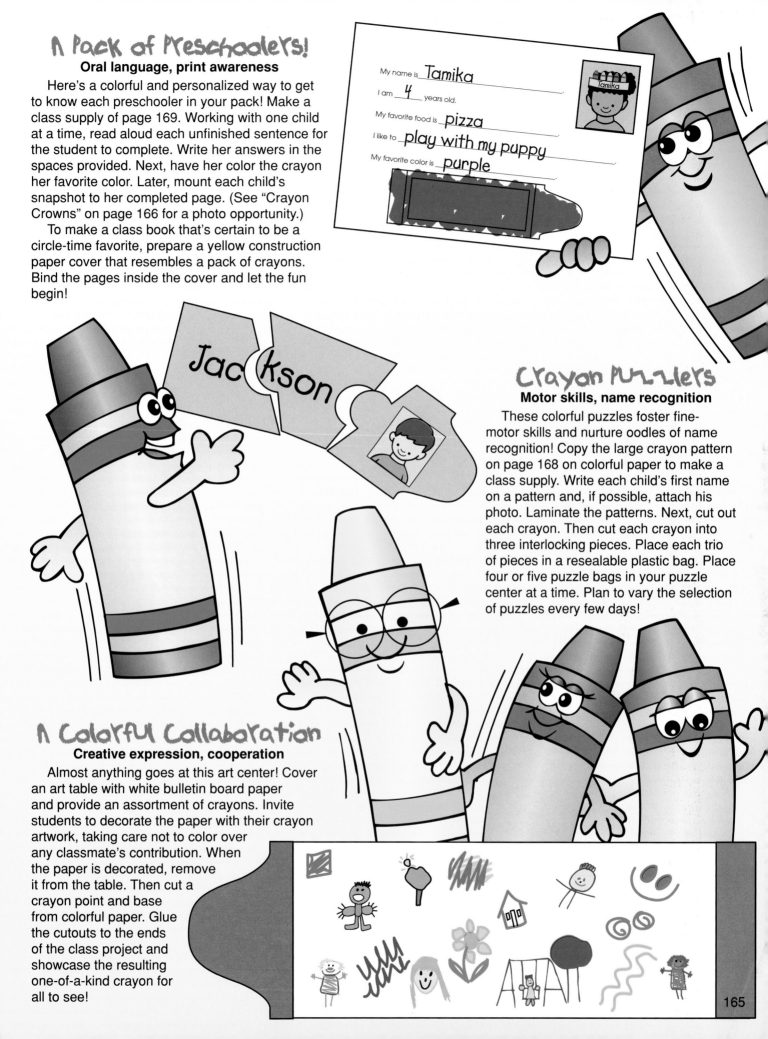

My name is **Tamika**
I am **4** years old.
My favorite food is **pizza**
I like to **play with my puppy**
My favorite color is **purple**

Crayon Puzzlers
Motor skills, name recognition

These colorful puzzles foster fine-motor skills and nurture oodles of name recognition! Copy the large crayon pattern on page 168 on colorful paper to make a class supply. Write each child's first name on a pattern and, if possible, attach his photo. Laminate the patterns. Next, cut out each crayon. Then cut each crayon into three interlocking pieces. Place each trio of pieces in a resealable plastic bag. Place four or five puzzle bags in your puzzle center at a time. Plan to vary the selection of puzzles every few days!

A Colorful Collaboration
Creative expression, cooperation

Almost anything goes at this art center! Cover an art table with white bulletin board paper and provide an assortment of crayons. Invite students to decorate the paper with their crayon artwork, taking care not to color over any classmate's contribution. When the paper is decorated, remove it from the table. Then cut a crayon point and base from colorful paper. Glue the cutouts to the ends of the class project and showcase the resulting one-of-a-kind crayon for all to see!

165

Crayon Crowns
Personal preferences

Preschoolers get royal treatment during this crown-making activity! Write each child's name near the center of a two-inch-wide strip of construction paper or bulletin board border. Also cut out (patterns on page 168) or die-cut a generous supply of crayon shapes from a variety of colored construction paper. Invite each child, one at a time, to a designated work area. Ask him to choose his five favorite crayon colors from the collection of cutouts and then glue the shapes to the blank side of his paper strip as shown. Provide assistance as needed to assure that the cutouts are glued upright and near the center of the strip. Later, when the glue is dry, have each youngster return to the work area. Size his paper headband to fit and then staple the ends. If desired, photograph each child wearing his crown. Then gather the crown-wearing youngsters in your circle-time area for some colorful chanting! (See "Hear This Cheer!" on this page.)

Hear This Cheer!
Self-concept

Promote positive self-concepts and a sense of community with this cheerful chant! Each time the chant is repeated, name a different child. Repeat the chant until each preschooler in the group has been named!

Glad You're Here!

All: Red and yellow, green and blue.
Teacher: [Child's name], [child's name], where are you?
(Named child raises hand.)
Teacher and peers: Look and listen; hear our cheer. We are glad that you are here!
(Teacher and peers wave to named child.)

TEC61166

Crayon Patterns

Use the large crayon with "Look Who's Here!" on page 164 and "Crayon Puzzlers" on page 165.

Use the small crayons with "Crayon Crowns" on page 166.

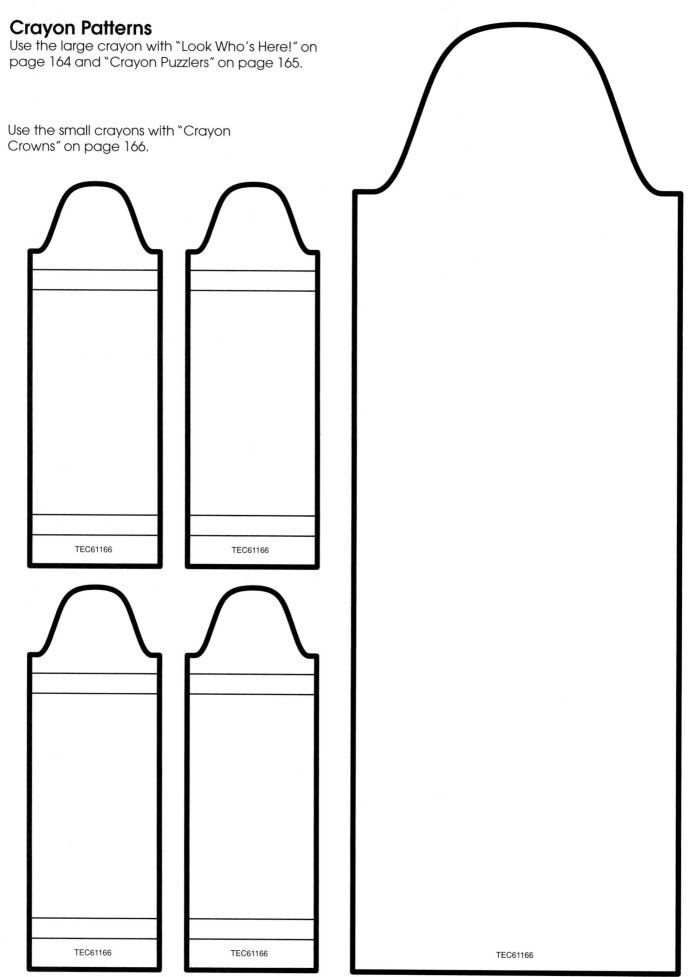

TEC61166

TEC61166

TEC61166

TEC61166

TEC61166

The Best of The Mailbox® Preschool • ©The Mailbox® Books • TEC61166

My name is _____

I am _____ years old.

My favorite food is _____

I like to _____

My favorite color is _____

~o the teacher: Use with "A Pack of Preschoolers!" on page 165.

Fire Safety—a Hot Topic

Calling all junior firefighters! These clever ideas help your little ones become knowledgeable about firefighters and fire safety.

ideas by Jana Sanderson—PreK, Rainbow School, Stockton, CA

One Firefighter Went Out to Spray

After teaching youngsters this catchy rhyme, invite students to pretend to be firefighters. Choose a child to be the first firefighter. Have him hold a long jump rope (hose) as the first verse is recited. When another firefighter is called to join him, instruct the two to walk around the room pretending to spray a fire while saying the rhyme. The last firefighter to join the line calls the next firefighter until all the children are walking around the room. After all children are holding the hose, have them recite the last verse.

[One] firefighter(s) went out to spray
Water on a red-orange flame one day.
The fire got big and hot that day.
So [he] called a friend to help [him] spray.

All the firefighters went out to spray
Water on a red-orange flame one day.
The big, hot fire was soon put out
By the brave firefighters, without a doubt!

Flashy Fire Hats

Children will be fired up to make these colorful hats to wear as you study fire safety. To prepare, cut thin strips of red, yellow, and orange tissue paper and metallic gift wrap. Make enough copies of the firefighter badges on page 173 so that each child will have one. Cut an 18" x 24" length of Con-Tact covering for each child. Pull back one half of the paper backing to expose a 12" x 18" sticky area. Tape the corners of the covering to a table to prevent it from moving. Have each child color and cut out a badge and add it facedown to his project as shown. Then instruct each youngster to cut the prepared strips into little pieces, allowing them to fall on the sticky surface. When each child has finished cutting the strips, pull off the remaining paper backing and fold the covering over the project. Cut each child's Con-Tact covering as shown to make a firefighter's hat. Encourage youngsters to sport their hats while completing the remaining activities in this unit.

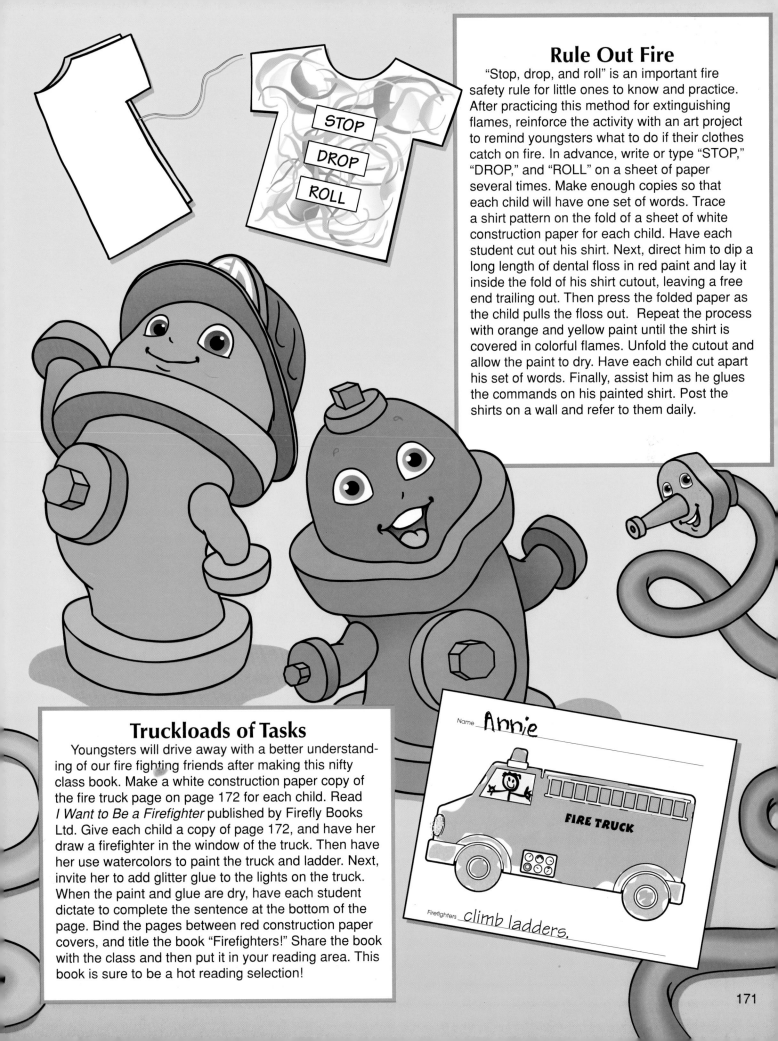

Rule Out Fire

"Stop, drop, and roll" is an important fire safety rule for little ones to know and practice. After practicing this method for extinguishing flames, reinforce the activity with an art project to remind youngsters what to do if their clothes catch on fire. In advance, write or type "STOP," "DROP," and "ROLL" on a sheet of paper several times. Make enough copies so that each child will have one set of words. Trace a shirt pattern on the fold of a sheet of white construction paper for each child. Have each student cut out his shirt. Next, direct him to dip a long length of dental floss in red paint and lay it inside the fold of his shirt cutout, leaving a free end trailing out. Then press the folded paper as the child pulls the floss out. Repeat the process with orange and yellow paint until the shirt is covered in colorful flames. Unfold the cutout and allow the paint to dry. Have each child cut apart his set of words. Finally, assist him as he glues the commands on his painted shirt. Post the shirts on a wall and refer to them daily.

Truckloads of Tasks

Youngsters will drive away with a better understanding of our fire fighting friends after making this nifty class book. Make a white construction paper copy of the fire truck page on page 172 for each child. Read *I Want to Be a Firefighter* published by Firefly Books Ltd. Give each child a copy of page 172, and have her draw a firefighter in the window of the truck. Then have her use watercolors to paint the truck and ladder. Next, invite her to add glitter glue to the lights on the truck. When the paint and glue are dry, have each student dictate to complete the sentence at the bottom of the page. Bind the pages between red construction paper covers, and title the book "Firefighters!" Share the book with the class and then put it in your reading area. This book is sure to be a hot reading selection!

Fire Truck Page

Use with "Truckloads of Tasks" on page 171.

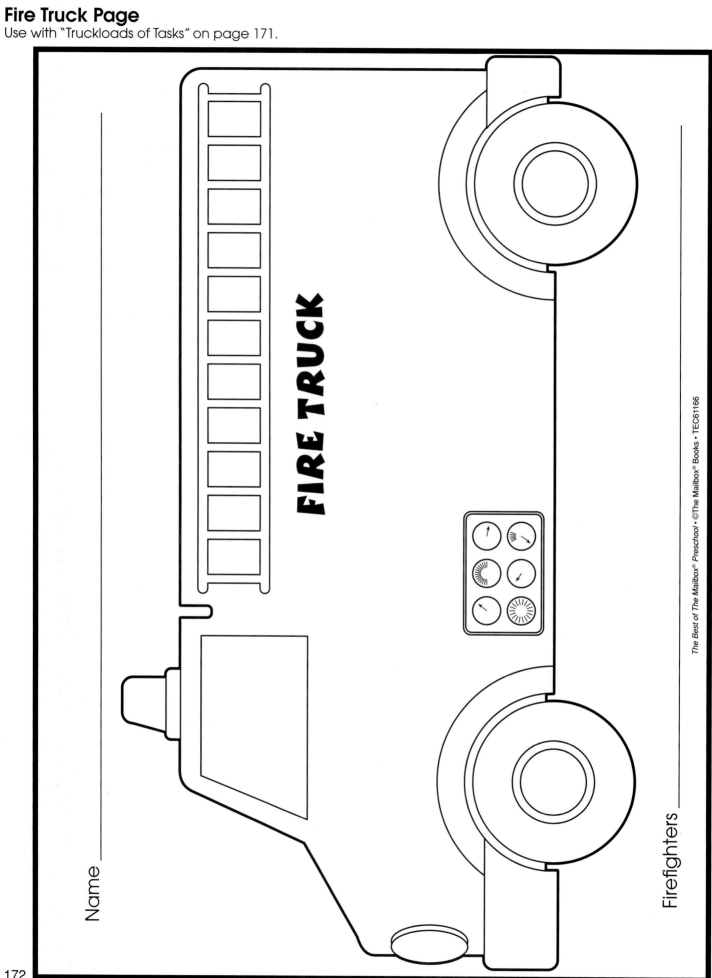

FIRE TRUCK

Name

Firefighters

The Best of The Mailbox® Preschool® •©The Mailbox® Books • TEC61166

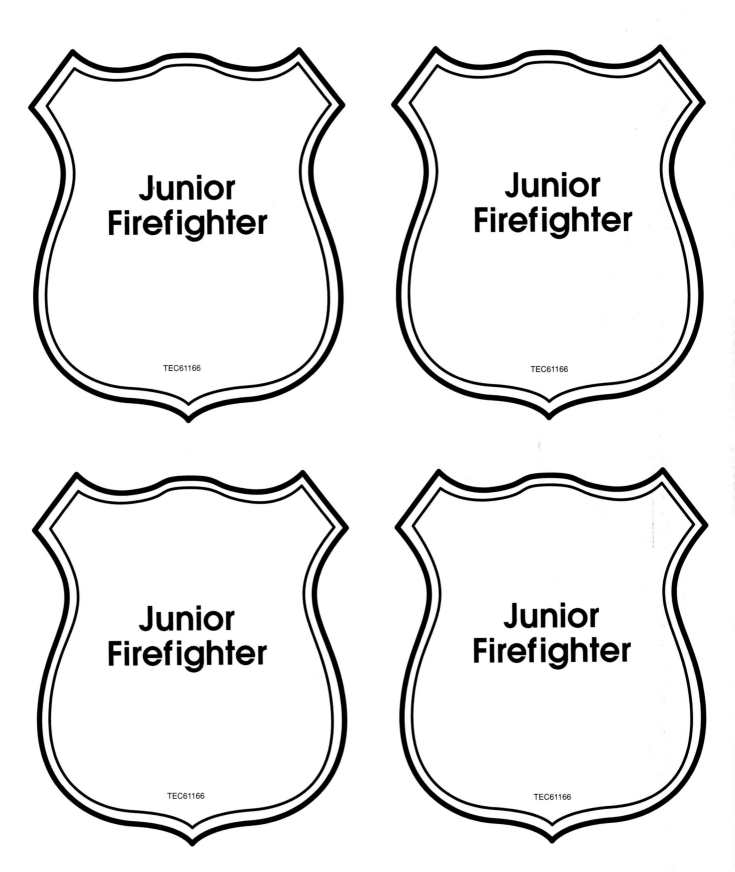

Junior Firefighter

TEC61166

Junior Firefighter

TEC61166

Junior Firefighter

TEC61166

Junior Firefighter

TEC61166

Plentiful Pumpkins!

Peruse this pumpkin patch and harvest a
bumper crop of learning opportunities. No
doubt the result will be oodles of cheery grins!

ideas contributed by Ada Goren, Winston-Salem, NC

What Is It?
Singing a song
Spotlight pumpkins with this divine little ditty! Make an orange
pumpkin cutout for each child plus one for yourself. Place the pumpkin
behind your back and sing to your youngsters the song shown, omit-
ting the spoken line at the end. Have students guess the object that the
song describes. When they guess that the item is a pumpkin, reveal
the cutout. Next, give each child her own cutout and have her hide it
behind her back. Then lead students in singing the song, having them
add the final spoken line as they reveal their own hidden pumpkins!

Suzanne Moore, Irving, TX

(sung to the tune of "Six Little Ducks")

I'm very orange and I am round.
I grew from a seed down in the ground.
You can carve me a face or put me in a pie.
Now take a guess and tell me,
What am I? What am I? What am I?
Now take a guess and tell me, what am I?

(spoken) A pumpkin!

In Line on the Vine
Ordering numerals
Make five orange construction paper pumpkins. Label each pumpkin
with a different numeral from 1 to 5 and the corresponding number of
dots. Also label each of five index cards in the same manner. Tape to a
flat surface a length of green yarn (vine) and green construction paper
leaves. Then tape the index cards in order along the vine. Place the
prepared pumpkins nearby. A child puts the matching pumpkin on top
of each index card to arrange the pumpkins from 1 to 5. For more ad-
vanced students, omit the index cards from the activity.

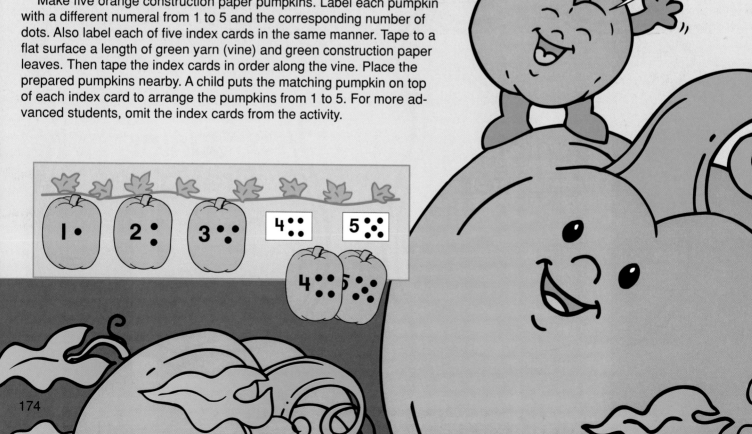

A Prizewinning Patch
Developing fine-motor skills

Youngsters create a pleasing pumpkin patch mural with prints made from miniature pumpkins! Tape a length of bulletin board paper to a table. Cut a miniature pumpkin in half and place the halves, cut side down, in a shallow pan of orange tempera paint. Place the pan at the table. Next, invite one or two youngsters to the table and encourage them to make several prints on the paper. Repeat the process until each child in the room has had an opportunity to make prints. When the paint is dry, invite students to cut green construction paper leaves and then glue them to the paper. Embellish the patch with green curling ribbon to resemble vines. Then post this nifty mural on a wall in your classroom!

Pass the Pumpkin
Listening for beginning sound /p/

Harvest phonemic awareness skills with this circle-time idea! Cut out a copy of the picture cards on page 176; then place them in a plastic trick-or-treat pumpkin. Gather students in a circle. Have youngsters pass the pumpkin around the circle as you lead them in singing the song shown. When the song is finished, locate the child holding the pumpkin and encourage him to remove a card. Have the student name the picture. Then instruct all the youngsters to say the name of the picture, emphasizing the /p/ sound at the beginning of the name. Continue in the same way for each card in the pumpkin.

(sung to the tune of "Clementine")

Pass the pumpkin, pass the pumpkin,
Pass the pumpkin round to me.
When it stops, I'll take out something
That begins with letter *P*!

pie

Picture Cards

Use with "Pass the Pumpkin" on page 175.

TEC61166

TEC61166

TEC61166

TEC61166

TEC61166

TEC61166

TEC61166

TEC61166

TEC61166

The Best of The Mailbox® Preschool • ©The Mailbox® Books • TEC61166

Families Are Fabulous!

Who are the most important people in your preschoolers' lives? Why, their families, of course! Invite little ones to focus on families for this selection of engaging learning opportunities!

ideas contributed by Roxanne LaBell Dearman, Western NC Early Intervention Program for Children Who Are Deaf or Hard of Hearing, Charlotte, NC

Counting on Families!
Counting and comparing numbers

Showcase the number of people in your young-sters' families with this picture-perfect idea! In advance, have each child bring in a photograph of his whole family. (To ensure the safety of the photos, place each one in a plastic bag or make a copy of the photo and send home the original.) Label each of six index cards as shown. Then display them in order at student eye level. Help each student count the total number of family members in his photo and then post it above the corresponding number. Encourage youngsters to compare the different family sizes using words such as *more, less,* and *same.*

Mealtime!
Engaging in dramatic play

Have each child name a favorite family meal and then draw the food on a large paper plate. Help her label each food pictured. Then place the completed plates at a table along with plastic utensils, napkins, and plastic serving dishes. Encourage center visitors to sit around the table and act like a family as they serve and feast on some favorite foods!

177

Chores Galore
Recognizing differences among families

It takes an entire family to run a household! Color and cut out a copy of the picture cards on page 179. To begin, show youngsters a card and invite them to name the chore pictured. Then encourage each child to discuss which member or members of his family complete that chore. Continue in this manner with each remaining card, making sure to highlight differences in youngsters' responses.

Dear Family,
    F is for family! Help your child decorate the provided letter cutout with photos, drawings, and objects that have meaning to your family. Please return the project to school by December 16.

Thank you,
Ms. Dearman

F Is for *Family!*
Building connections between home and school

Send home with each child a large uppercase *F* cutout and a note similar to the one shown. Encourage each child to help her family decorate the cutout with items that have special meaning. For example, they might add drawings of the family pet or pictures from a family vacation. When youngsters bring their projects to school, invite each child to share her unique *F*. No doubt you'll want to display these nifty projects for all to see!

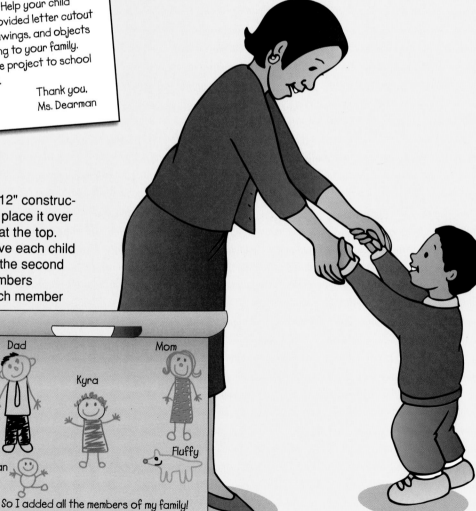

All in the Family
Naming family members

For each child, gather two sheets of 9" x 12" construction paper. Cut a window in one sheet; then place it over the second sheet and staple them together at the top. Label the papers with the rhyme shown. Have each child draw a self-portrait in the window. Then, on the second page, encourage her to draw her family members around her. Finally, help each child label each member of her family.

I drew a picture,
A picture of me.

But then I thought
I might be lonely, you see.

Dad   Kyra   Mom

Evan   Fluffy

So I added all the members of my family!

TEC61166

TEC61166

TEC61166

TEC61166

TOYS

TEC61166

TEC61166

'Tis the Season for Learning

Deck the halls with lots of learning…fa, la, la, la, la! Use the excitement of the season to help your little ones get hooked on learning using this ornament-related thematic unit.

ideas by Angie Kutzer, Garrett Elementary, Mebane, NC

Festive Letters

● *Observing the shapes of letters* ●

Make learning letters more festive with this decorative idea. Program a sheet of construction paper for each child with her first initial. Provide her with a bingo dauber to dot over the penciled lines. Then show each child how to draw a hook on several dots to create ornaments. Invite each child to share her letter with the class. For added interest, provide youngsters with holiday stickers to decorate the areas around their letters. Bind the pages between construction paper covers and title the book "Festive Letters."

A Perfect Pick

● *Using vocabulary, visual discrimination* ●

Reinforce the use of descriptive vocabulary with this circle-time guessing game. Place an assortment of eight to 12 ornaments in front of youngsters. Secretly choose one to describe. For example, you might say, "I see an ornament that is flat. It's shiny. It has curvy lines." With each new clue, pause a moment to allow youngsters to look over the collection. After giving your description, encourage students to point to the appropriate ornament. Then start again with a new ornament description. After youngsters understand the game, invite a volunteer to describe an ornament of his choice. Continue play until each child has had a turn.

I'm a Little Ornament
● *Singing a song* ●

Sing this quick song with your little ones to get those wintry wiggles out and get youngsters ready for learning!

(sung to the tune of "I'm a Little Teapot")

I'm a shiny ornament, big and round.
I'm hanging on the tree while watching the ground.
When the children come in with a bound,
I dance and wiggle to their joyful sound!

Hold arms out in front, making a big circle.
Put hand above eyes as if searching below.
Jump.
Sway back and forth.

Jump
12
times.

Countdown to Christmas
● *Reviewing skills* ●

This "undecorating" idea leads to lots of fun skills review. To prepare, cut out a large tree shape from green bulletin board paper and mount it near your calendar. Make several colorful construction paper copies of the ornament patterns on page 183 so that you will have one pattern for each school day in December. Program each cutout with a different activity, such as "Sing the alphabet," "Jump 12 times," or "Name your favorite color." Cut out the patterns and attach them to the tree. Each day during calendar time, have a different student remove an ornament from the tree. Read the activity aloud and encourage youngsters to complete the given task. Just a few more days to go!

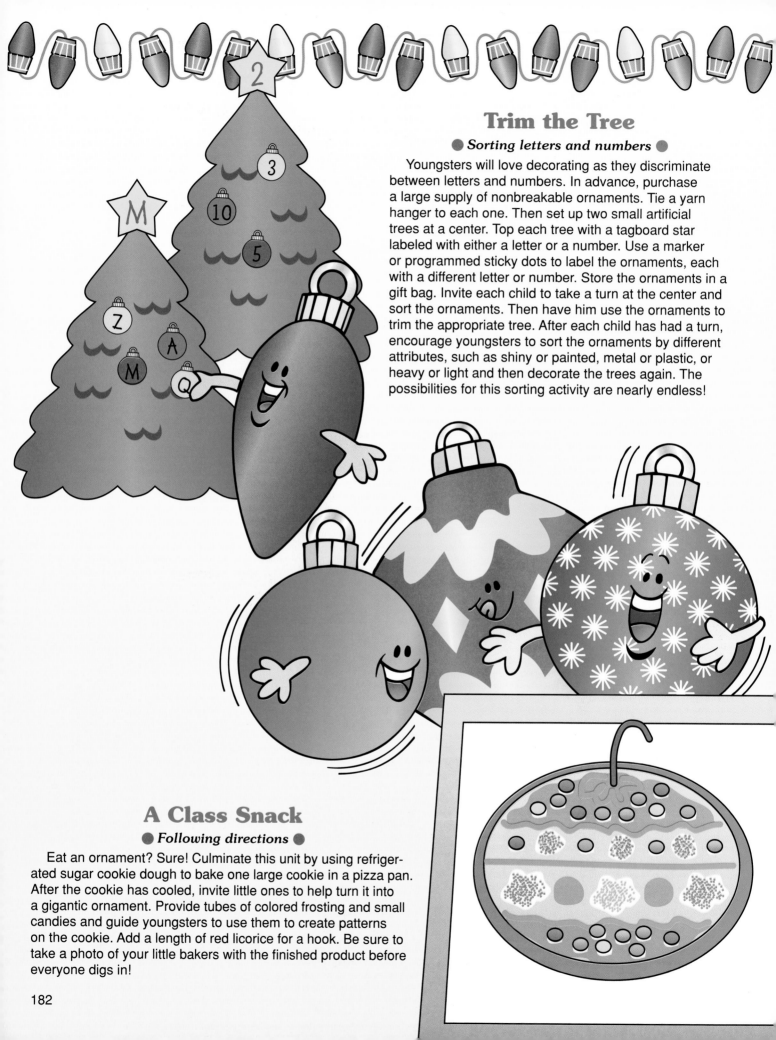

Trim the Tree

● *Sorting letters and numbers* ●

Youngsters will love decorating as they discriminate between letters and numbers. In advance, purchase a large supply of nonbreakable ornaments. Tie a yarn hanger to each one. Then set up two small artificial trees at a center. Top each tree with a tagboard star labeled with either a letter or a number. Use a marker or programmed sticky dots to label the ornaments, each with a different letter or number. Store the ornaments in a gift bag. Invite each child to take a turn at the center and sort the ornaments. Then have him use the ornaments to trim the appropriate tree. After each child has had a turn, encourage youngsters to sort the ornaments by different attributes, such as shiny or painted, metal or plastic, or heavy or light and then decorate the trees again. The possibilities for this sorting activity are nearly endless!

A Class Snack

● *Following directions* ●

Eat an ornament? Sure! Culminate this unit by using refrigerated sugar cookie dough to bake one large cookie in a pizza pan. After the cookie has cooled, invite little ones to help turn it into a gigantic ornament. Provide tubes of colored frosting and small candies and guide youngsters to use them to create patterns on the cookie. Add a length of red licorice for a hook. Be sure to take a photo of your little bakers with the finished product before everyone digs in!

TEC61166

TEC61166

TEC61166

TEC61166

Hooray for Valentine's Day!

Celebrate Valentine's Day in a big way with this colossal collection of ideas!

ideas contributed by Ada Goren, Winston-Salem, NC

Make a Match
Matching letters
When youngsters play this small-group game, they're in for a real treat! To prepare, gather an empty heart-shaped candy box and write pairs of letters on the inside in a random arrangement. Press a small ball of brown play dough (chocolate) on top of each letter. To begin, gather a small group of youngsters around the box. Each student takes a turn removing two chocolates. If the letters match, he keeps the chocolates. If they do not match, he returns the chocolates to the box. Play continues until all of the letter pairs are uncovered.

Dino Decor
Developing fine-motor skills
Enlarge the dinosaur pattern on page 188 and make a construction paper copy for each child. Cut out the dinosaurs. Prepare a supply of small construction paper heart cutouts. Invite each child to glue the hearts upside down along the spine and tail of the dinosaur to resemble bony plates. Personalize each dinosaur and then display the completed projects on a bulletin board titled "Valentine's Day Is 'Dino-mite'!"

Emily

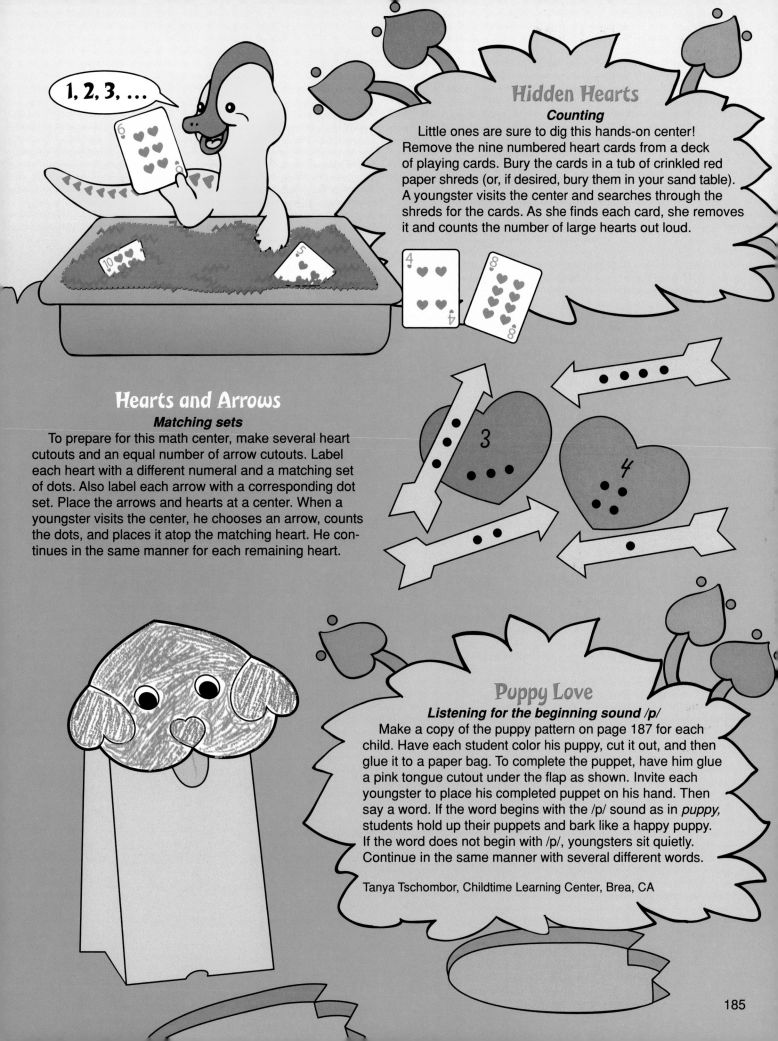

Hidden Hearts
Counting
Little ones are sure to dig this hands-on center! Remove the nine numbered heart cards from a deck of playing cards. Bury the cards in a tub of crinkled red paper shreds (or, if desired, bury them in your sand table). A youngster visits the center and searches through the shreds for the cards. As she finds each card, she removes it and counts the number of large hearts out loud.

Hearts and Arrows
Matching sets
To prepare for this math center, make several heart cutouts and an equal number of arrow cutouts. Label each heart with a different numeral and a matching set of dots. Also label each arrow with a corresponding dot set. Place the arrows and hearts at a center. When a youngster visits the center, he chooses an arrow, counts the dots, and places it atop the matching heart. He continues in the same manner for each remaining heart.

Puppy Love
Listening for the beginning sound /p/
Make a copy of the puppy pattern on page 187 for each child. Have each student color his puppy, cut it out, and then glue it to a paper bag. To complete the puppet, have him glue a pink tongue cutout under the flap as shown. Invite each youngster to place his completed puppet on his hand. Then say a word. If the word begins with the /p/ sound as in *puppy,* students hold up their puppets and bark like a happy puppy. If the word does not begin with /p/, youngsters sit quietly. Continue in the same manner with several different words.

Tanya Tschombor, Childtime Learning Center, Brea, CA

Hugs and Kisses

Making a pattern

Place at a center a supply of construction paper strips, a shallow pan of tempera paint, and X and O sponge stamps (or use a stamp pad and X and O rubber stamps). Explain to students that Xs and Os represent hugs and kisses. Then invite students to visit the center and stamp a simple pattern along a strip. Use the completed strips as bulletin board border or cut the strips into smaller pieces to make snazzy bracelets!

Leslie Boyett
Asbury Ark Academy
Bossier City, LA

Love Potion

Following directions

Give each child a scoop of raspberry sherbet in a clear plastic cup. Help her pour a half cup of lemon-lime soda over the sherbet. Then have her add a dollop of whipped cream to her drink. For added fun, invite each child to top her drink with a dash of heart-shaped sprinkles.

Please Be Mine

Participating in a song

No doubt little ones will just love this toe-tapping tune. It's perfect for a Valentine's Day celebration!

(sung to the tune of "Bingo")

My friend gave me a valentine.
Its message is so fine!
Won't you please be mine?
Won't you please be mine?
Won't you please be mine?
Please be my valentine!

adapted from an idea by Suzanne Moore
Tucson, AZ

The Queen's Tarts
Contributing to a class book

This twist on a traditional nursery rhyme is the inspiration for a nifty class book! To begin, explain that a tart is a filled pastry similar to a pie. Then lead students in reciting the rhyme shown. Next, give each child a copy of page 189 and invite him to describe what surprising filling the queen put in one of her tarts. Write each student's response along the bottom of his paper. Then have him decorate the tart to match. Bind youngsters' completed papers together behind a cover labeled with the rhyme.

The Queen of Hearts, she made some tarts
To sell at the bake sale for me.
They were all different sizes
And full of surprises.
Oh, what a good baker was she!

Name _Ethan_ _____ Writing

One tart was filled with _spaghetti_
and cookies!

Puppy Pattern
Use with "Puppy Love" on page 185.

TEC61166

Dinosaur Pattern

Use with "Yikes! Spikes!" on page 49
and "Dino Decor" on page 184.

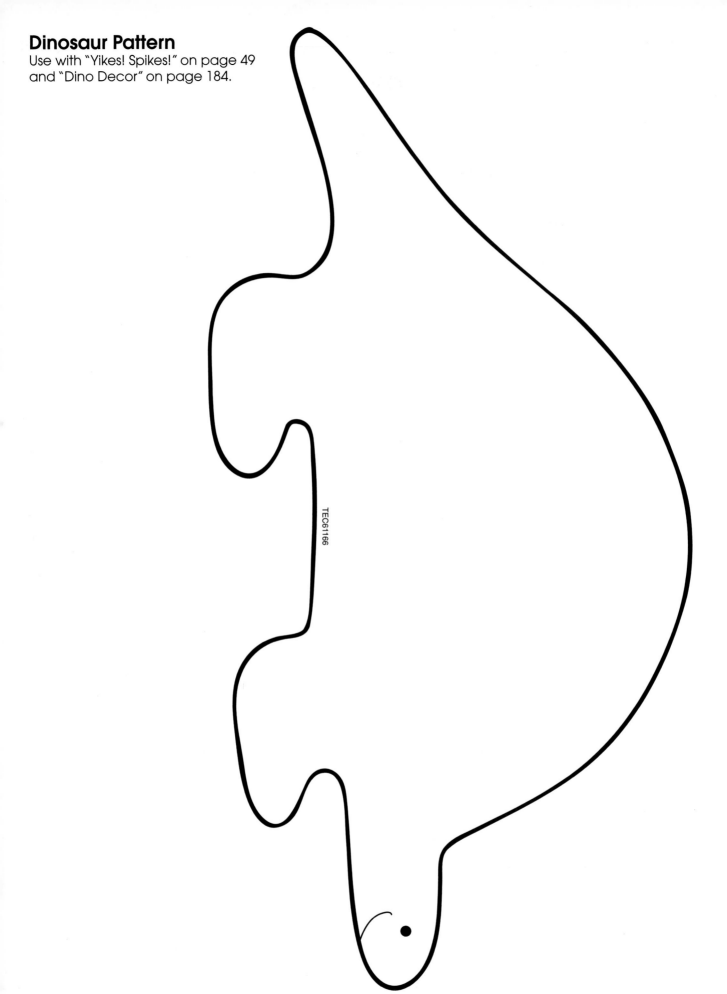

TEC61166

The Best of The Mailbox® • *Preschool* • ©The Mailbox® Books • TEC61166

Time for Tarts

One tart was filled with _____

_____

Topic and Skills Index